SAM THE COOKING GUY

SAM THE COOKING GUY

RECIPES WITH INTENTIONAL LEFTOVERS

SAM ZIEN

The Countryman Press
A Division of W. W. Norton & Company
Independent Publishers Since 1923

Copyright © 2020 by Sam Zien
Photography by Lucas Barbieri

For information about permission to reproduce selections from this book,
write to Permissions, The Countryman Press, 500 Fifth Avenue, New York, NY 10110

For information about special discounts for bulk purchases, please contact
W. W. Norton Special Sales at specialsales@wwnorton.com or 800-233-4830

Manufactured by Versa Press
Book design by Allison Chi
Production manager: Devon Zahn

The Countryman Press
www.countrymanpress.com

A division of W. W. Norton & Company, Inc.
500 Fifth Avenue, New York, NY 10110
www.wwnorton.com

978-1-68268-602-7 (pbk.)

10 9 8 7 6 5 4 3 2

Dedicated to . . .

That leftover piece of pizza, the forgotten slice of meatloaf, or the handful of stray meatballs no one finished.

Forget what they say about you being "no good anymore." You guys are as important and meaningful today as the day you were made . . . maybe even more so. Because with a little love and care, you'll come back to life better, more delicious, and often way more interesting than your first time around.

You just needed someone to believe.

THANK YOU TO . . .

- Kelly—for everything always, forever and ever
- The Boys—with a major foghorn
- Michael—for reaching out way back
- Leigh—for jumping in way back
- Lucas—for your photos, your patience, and your ideas
- Beth—for your testing, tasting, and everything else
- The Shuneems—for just being yourselves
- Everyone who bought this
- And to anyone who's looking at this right now in a store or online and wondering whether you should buy it, to you I say, go on—it's a damn good book, and I think you'll really like it.

CONTENTS

LEFTOVERS, REALLY?

THIRTY-EIGHT MILLION POUNDS of leftovers are thrown out every day in North America, and that's just wrong. And it's also BS cuz I just made it up. But you know that, whatever the number is, it's fricking huge—and that just doesn't have to happen.

Everyone likes leftovers. In fact, many would argue it's all about the leftovers. Because having a steak with mashed potatoes one night and then exactly the same way the next couple of nights is so boring. So, instead, how 'bout we turn those into a mashed potato and steak pizza with smoked Gouda? Or a beautifully roasted chicken one night becomes taquitos or a crazy good Thai curry on rice the next. And because the possibilities are pretty much endless, you'll find yourself fighting for the doggie bag at a restaurant, asking your hosts for a little take-home gift or at least throwing a couple extra pieces of chicken on the grill.

#LEFTOVERSRULE

Some Things to Note

1. You should always read a recipe all the way through before starting.

2. You also should probably not make a recipe the very first time for someone you're trying to impress. Of course I think my stuff is simple to make, but you never know what'll go wrong, and a test drive can never be a bad thing.

3. Any place you read "salt," I mean kosher or sea salt. While both are pure with no additives, sea salt is more expensive to make, hence it's more expensive to buy. Virtually every restaurant kitchen uses kosher salt for the majority of its cooking, and the prettier, flakier sea salt for presentation. Me, too. This also means you can get rid of any table salt in favor of kosher or sea salt.

4. And any place you read "oil," I mean a neutral, unflavored oil. Ideally, you'll be using avocado oil, as it has the highest smoke point, is very clean tasting, and is a source of good fat. If I want you to use a flavored oil, I'll tell you.

5. And any place you read "butter," I mean regular, salted butter. I only keep salted butter—and no, my recipes are not salty. To me, unsalted butter is a ruse perpetrated on us by the baking community to make them feel superior with their special butter. Let them keep their two butter options—you and me will stick to salted. Plus, you'll never have the problem of accidentally using unsalted butter on a piece of toast, which is a horrifying experience.

6. And any place you read "grease a pan," you can use butter, oil, or cooking spray.

7. Below the servings for each recipe is an estimate of preparation and cooking time—roughly what I think it should take to make it. If you're a slowpoke, add more time. If you're really chatty while you cook and can only do one thing at a time, add even more time. And since no one likes a last-minute race, remember that a lot of prep can be done in advance, even a day or so before in many cases.

8. Because I will have no idea how much of anything you might have left over, some recipes may be slightly less detailed and may be more of a suggestion.

9. In other cases, again because we're talking leftovers, instead of specifying exactly how much a recipe will make, I might use "MBOWYG," which means "measurements based on what you've got."

10. Cooking with someone is waaaaaay more fun than cooking alone—so get someone and get cooking. And if you're in one of those relationships where one person cooks and the other doesn't . . . the one who doesn't better effing well clear and do dishes. Cuz that's just how it goes.

11. And, finally, the only way you get better at *anything* is by practicing. The first time you try a recipe (mine or anyone's), it might not turn out all that well. But make it a second time, and now you know stuff. Like maybe your oven at 425°F is really more like 375°F and what you cooked came out a little underdone. That's not you—that's the oven. So turn it up a bit or have it calibrated. Maybe the recipe said 1 cup of sugar and that was too sweet for you—just use less the second time around. I wasn't there the first time you rode a bike, but I'm pretty sure you fell—and now you can ride. And the only difference between then and now is practice.

MEATBALLS, AND THEN . . .

No laughing—this is not a
silly chapter. You'll like the
outcomes so much you'll be making
meatballs every week. Plus,
I just don't think people are
making meatballs often enough,
and that's a shame.

Meatballs
Glorious Meatball Pho
Pesto French Bread Pizza
Cheesy Hand Meatballs
Meatball Banh Mi
Meatball Greek Salad

MEATBALLS

MAKES ABOUT 12 MEATBALLS

30 MINUTES

No cute name, just a damn good meatball made even lovelier by the addition of ricotta cheese. And my very strong suggestion is for you to make at least a double batch and freeze them. Because remembering you have meatballs in your freezer is like remembering on Sunday that it's a long weekend and you have tomorrow off.

8 ounces ground beef

8 ounces ground pork

8 ounces ground veal

½ cup ricotta

⅓ cup shredded Parmesan

½ cup panko bread crumbs

2 large garlic cloves, minced

1 teaspoon kosher salt

1 teaspoon freshly ground black pepper*

½ teaspoon red pepper flakes

1 large egg

1. Preheat the oven to 400°F.

2. Put everything into a large bowl and mix well—with your hands please, not a spoon.

3. Roll into balls and place on a parchment-lined baking sheet.

4. Bake for about 15 minutes, or until cooked all the way through.

5. Boom.

*I was going to shorten "freshly ground black pepper" to "FGBP"—but that sounded like something the spawn of Rachael Ray and Guy Fieri might say, so I won't.

GLORIOUS MEATBALL PHO

SERVES 4
25 MINUTES

Wikipedia say that pho is usually a "Vietnamese soup consisting of broth, rice noodles, herbs, and meat—usually beef." Nowhere does it say pho has to be uncooked sliced beef—which it often is. I love this, I love the broth, I love the whole thing. And since you have some meatballs in the freezer (because you listened), you can just slip them into the broth frozen and they'll come perfectly back to life in about 10 minutes.

32 ounces beef stock

2 star anise

3 limes

One 1-inch piece fresh
    ginger, cut into 4 slices

8 ounces rice noodles

8 leftover Meatballs (page 14),
    warmed slightly in
    a microwave

One 8-ounce bag bean sprouts

1 bunch green onions, white
    and light green parts only,
    sliced into thin strips

1 big handful fresh cilantro

1 small red chile, sliced
    very thinly

Hoisin sauce for serving

Sriracha for serving

1. Combine the stock, star anise, the juice of two of the limes, and the ginger in a medium pot. Bring to a boil, lower the heat slightly, and simmer for about 15 minutes.

2. Bring a large pot of water to a boil, add the noodles, and cook for 3 minutes.

3. Drain the noodles well and divide among four bowls.

4. Add the meatballs and cover with the stock.

5. Then add some bean sprouts, green onion, cilantro, red chile, and a squeeze of juice from one-quarter of the remaining lime to each bowl.

6. Add some hoisin and sriracha to taste to each bowl and eat.

7. Damn, it's so good.

PESTO FRENCH BREAD PIZZA

SERVES 4 TO 6

10 MINUTES

This is a huge family favorite. So much so that I have a flatbread version of this pizza on the menu of my restaurant, Graze.

2 tablespoons butter

1 large garlic clove, minced

2 tablespoons all-purpose flour

1 cup milk

¼ cup grated or shredded Parmesan

10 leftover Meatballs (page 14), cut into 4 or 5 slices each

½ cup basil pesto

One 11- to 12-inch loaf French bread

1 cup grated mozzarella

1. Heat the butter in a medium pot over low heat, and when melted, add the garlic.

2. Cook for about a minute, or until just fragrant, then sprinkle with the flour and whisk to incorporate.*

3. Continue to cook, stirring, for about a minute, or until the mixture becomes superdry.

4. Slowly add the milk, whisking to incorporate (there it is again).

5. When it's mixed, add the Parmesan and stir well until thick and smooth.

6. Preheat the broiler.

7. Cut the French bread lengthwise and add a generous layer of the cheese sauce to both cut sides.

8. Place the cut meatballs in a bowl and microwave on HIGH for about 20 seconds, or until just warm. Add the pesto and toss to mix through.

9. Put a layer of the meatballs on the cheese sauce and top with mozzarella.

10. Place under the broiler and broil until bubbly, melty, and gorgeous.

11. Slice and serve.

*Pretty sure I've never used the term *incorporate* in a recipe's directions before and was thinking of replacing it, but it kind of makes me sound smart . . . or at least a little Martha Stewart-ish, and I kind of like that. It's a good thing.

CHEESY HAND MEATBALLS

MAKES 12 HAND MEATBALLS
25 MINUTES

Beautiful pizza dough lovingly wrapped around a delicious meatball that you can hold in your hand and eat like an apple. A drippy, messy apple that'll get sauce and crumbs everywhere. Let's rethink that metaphor . . .

1 pound pizza dough

¾ cup shredded cheese, pizza blend, or mozzarella

1½ cups leftover Roasted Red Pepper Sauce (page 180), plus more for serving

12 leftover Meatballs (page 14)

Chopped fresh basil for garnish

1. Preheat the oven to 400°F. Lightly grease a 12-well muffin pan with butter or cooking spray.

2. Spread the dough into approximately a 15-by-20-inch rectangle, cut into twelve 4-inch circles, then press one circle into each prepared muffin well.

3. Put about 1 tablespoon of cheese and 1 tablespoon of red pepper sauce into each dough-lined well, and then add a meatball.

4. Add more sauce to the top, then more cheese.

5. Bake for about 15 minutes, or until the dough is crispy and the cheese is melted.

6. Garnish with basil and serve with extra sauce for dipping.

MEATBALL BANH MI

While there's no roast pork or pâté in this, you'll still get that delicious banh mi flavor. And they're pretty as a picture, aren't they?

2 tablespoons rice vinegar

1 teaspoon sugar

⅓ cup carrot, cut into matchsticks

⅓ cup cucumber, unpeeled and cut into matchsticks

Pinch of kosher salt

Four 8-inch long crusty baguettes

½ cup Japanese mayonnaise

2 tablespoons sriracha

½ teaspoon sesame oil

12 leftover Meatballs (page 14)

½ cup hoisin sauce

Sesame seeds for garnish

Cilantro for garnish

1. Put the rice vinegar and sugar in a small bowl, mix to combine, and add the carrots and cucumber. Season with a pinch of salt and let sit for 30 minutes.

2. Cut the rolls lengthwise down the middle, leaving a hinge.

3. Combine the mayo, sriracha, and sesame oil in a small bowl, then spread generously down the middle of each roll. Add some of the carrots and cucumber, shaking off excess liquid.

4. Toss the meatballs with the hoisin sauce in a medium bowl and microwave on MEDIUM HIGH for 1 minute.

5. Add 3 meatballs to each roll, along with any remaining carrot and cucumber, then garnish with sesame seeds and cilantro.

MEATBALL GREEK SALAD

There's a steak salad, a chicken salad, and even a lovely salmon salad. Who says there can't be a meatball salad?

¼ cup olive oil

2 tablespoons red wine vinegar

2 teaspoons Dijon mustard

2 teaspoons dried oregano

1 clove garlic, minced

½ teaspoon sugar

4 medium ripe vine tomatoes,
   cut into wedges

2 Persian cucumbers,
   sliced into thin rounds

½ red onion, sliced thin

½ cup pitted Kalamata
   olives, cut in half

½ cup crumbled feta cheese

Kosher salt and freshly ground
   black pepper to taste

12 leftover Meatballs (page 14)

1. Combine the olive oil, vinegar, mustard, oregano, garlic, and sugar in a small bowl. Thoroughly mix the dressing and set aside.

2. Put the tomatoes, cucumber, onion, olives, and feta cheese in a large bowl and toss with the most of the dressing. Season with salt and pepper. Let sit for about 15 minutes.

3. Plate the salad, add the meatballs, and drizzle with the remaining dressing.

4. Serve immediately.

BEER—BRAISED SHORT RIBS, AND THEN . . .

You lift the lid when it's finished cooking and revel in the slow-braised steam that rises up to meet you. And if you haven't burned your nose, you'll realize that this is probably what heaven smells like. And the same delicate, richly flavored beef that you simply eat with a fork on day one becomes the wonderful leftovers below. If you've never actually danced for joy, you will now.

Beer-Braised Short Ribs
Easy Short Rib Stroganoff
Short Rib Egg Rolls
The Ultimate Cheesesteak

BEER-BRAISED SHORT RIBS

SERVES 4
3-ISH HOURS

This is a huge payoff for really just a little work. It's elegant, it's delicious, and it's stupidly impressive . . . and it's way easier than most people think.

4 pounds bone-in short ribs (about 8)

Kosher salt and freshly ground black pepper

2 tablespoons oil

4 carrots, cut into 1-inch pieces

4 celery stalks, cut into 1-inch pieces

1 small yellow onion, cut into medium dice

3 garlic cloves

3 tablespoons tomato paste

3 tablespoons all-purpose flour

2 cups beef stock

One 12-ounce bottle of your favorite dark beer, a stout, anything with big flavor

6 sprigs thyme

1. Preheat the oven to 300°F.

2. Season the short ribs well with salt and pepper.

3. Heat the oil in a heavy, ovenproof pot with a lid (such as a Dutch oven) over medium-high heat and sear the short ribs until browned on all sides (except the bone side). Transfer to a plate and set aside.

4. Add the carrots, celery, and onion to the pot and cook until just beginning to soften, about 3 minutes, then add the garlic and stir to combine, another minute.

5. Add the tomato paste and flour to the vegetables; stir well to combine and cook for another minute or so.

6. Add the beef stock and beer, stirring well to combine everything.

7. Bring to a boil, then turn off the heat and add the ribs back to the pot, along with the thyme.

8. Cover with the lid, put in the oven, and bake until fork-tender, 2½ to 3 hours.

9. Serve with the vegetables and some of the delicious gravy/broth from the pot on anything—mashed potatoes, rice, pasta, etc.

EASY SHORT RIB STROGANOFF

SERVES 2
15 MINUTES

Is there a person alive who doesn't appreciate rich, deeply flavored short ribs with onions and mushrooms atop those oh-so-cool wide egg noodles? If there is, I don't want to meet them.

3 tablespoons cornstarch

3 tablespoons cold water

1½ cups beef stock

2 tablespoons butter

½ medium onion, diced

8 ounces cremini mushrooms, stemmed and thinly sliced

Kosher salt and freshly ground black pepper

⅓ cup sour cream

1 teaspoon Worcestershire sauce

1 tablespoon prepared horseradish

1 tablespoon finely chopped fresh dill, plus more for garnish

8 ounces shredded leftover Beer-Braised Short Ribs (page 28)

1. Mix the cornstarch and cold water in a small bowl until very smooth.

2. Put the stock in a small pot over medium heat and, once warm, add the cornstarch slurry and stir or whisk until it thickens, then remove from the heat and set aside.

3. Melt the butter in a large skillet over medium heat, then cook the onion and mushrooms until lightly browned, 3 to 5 minutes. Season with salt and pepper to taste.

4. Add the thickened stock, sour cream, Worcestershire, horseradish, and dill. Stir to combine and add the short ribs. Let simmer for 5 minutes.

5. Serve over egg noodles, rice, or whatever makes sense, maybe with a little more dill for garnish.

SHORT RIB EGG ROLLS

MAKES 10 EGG ROLLS
60 MINUTES

Crispy, crunchy, savory—what more could you ask for? And once you know how to make these, almost anything can become an egg roll.

1 large yellow onion, diced

1 tablespoon oil, plus more for brushing

Kosher salt and freshly ground black pepper

1 cup shredded green cabbage, liquid squeezed out

1 cup shredded leftover Beer-Braised Short Ribs (page 28)

½ cup sour cream

½ cup Creole or coarse-grain mustard

1 tablespoon hot sauce, plus more for serving

10 egg roll wrappers

1. Preheat the oven to 400°F.

2. Cook the onion in the oil in a medium skillet over medium heat until nicely caramelized, about 7 minutes, then season with salt and pepper to taste.

3. Transfer the onion to a medium bowl and add the cabbage and short ribs. Mix together.

4. Mix together the sour cream, mustard, and hot sauce in a small bowl.

5. Lay out one egg roll wrapper with a corner pointed toward you. Place some of the short rib mixture in the center and spread a little mustard alongside it.

6. Fold the closest corner up over the mixture, pull it back slightly to make a relatively tight package, then fold the left and right corners toward the center and continue to roll away from you. Wet the underside of the final corner with a little water on your finger to help seal the egg roll, then repeat to fill the remaining wrappers.

7. Place the egg rolls on a parchment-lined baking sheet.

8. Brush the egg rolls really lightly with oil, then bake for 20 to 25 minutes, until golden brown.

9. Serve with extra hot sauce.

THE ULTIMATE CHEESESTEAK

MAKES 2 CHEESESTEAKS
10 MINUTES

The first time I made this I was nearly chased by villagers carrying torches like they went after Frankenstein's monster. Honestly, these fricking cheesesteak people cannot change one thing, or they go nuts. The whole "wit or witout" thing is a big enough deal on its own, but when you introduce a whole different meat . . . just look the hell out. Oh, and "wit or witout" is how you order onions or not on your cheesesteak in Philly.

1 tablespoon neutral oil

1 green bell pepper, seeded and thinly sliced

1 yellow onion, thinly sliced

8 ounces cremini mushrooms, stemmed and thinly sliced

8 ounces leftover Beer-Braised Short Ribs (page 28)

4 slices provolone, or 6 table-spoons processed cheese sauce, such as Cheez Whiz

2 crusty Italian-style sandwich rolls, split in half crosswise and lightly toasted

Kosher salt and freshly ground black pepper

1. Heat the oil in a large nonstick skillet or on a flat griddle over medium-high heat and cook the bell pepper, onion, and mushrooms until softened, 3 to 4 minutes.

2. Push the vegetables over to one side and add the short ribs. Season with salt and black pepper.

3. Using the oil already in the pan, your goal is to warm up the rib eye and short ribs nicely, so keep it moving.

4. Separate the vegetables into two long piles approximately the length of the rolls and top with the short ribs.

5. If using provolone, this is the time to add two slices to each pile. If using cheese sauce, warm it up in a microwave on HIGH for about 15 seconds, or until pourable.

6. If using provolone, slide a spatula under each pile and put it, cheese side up, on top of a toasted roll. If using cheese sauce, slide a spatula under each pile and put it on top of a toasted roll, then drizzle the cheese sauce beautifully on top.

7. You're done, except for the eating . . . and defending yourself from staunch cheesesteak traditionalists.

JEWISH-STYLE BRISKET, AND THEN . . .

Boy oh boy, I really like
this. And apart from being my
people's celebratory food of
choice (I mean, what Jewish
holiday wouldn't benefit from
a delicious brisket?), the
leftovers are simply the best
and stupidly versatile.

Jewish-Style Brisket
Brisket Fries with Spicy Cheese Sauce
World's Best Grilled Cheese
Brisket Empanadas

JEWISH-STYLE BRISKET

SERVES 6 TO 8
5 HOURS

I call it "Jewish" because brisket is the centerpiece of many Jewish holidays. And unlike a brisket cooked on a smoker, this one is made in the oven (and a great reason to buy a big Dutch oven if you don't already have one). And as great as it is for dinner, it's fantastic and arguably better the next day for everything else.

5 tablespoons oil
One 5- to 7-pound beef brisket
4 garlic cloves, minced
3 large yellow onions, thinly sliced
One 12-ounce can tomato paste
¾ cup brown sugar
½ cup soy sauce
2 tablespoons Dijon mustard
1 tablespoon smoked paprika
2 cups beef stock

1. Preheat the oven to 350°F.

2. Heat 2 tablespoons of the oil over medium-high heat in a heavy pot (such as cast iron or a Dutch oven) large enough to hold the brisket.

3. Add the brisket and brown on both sides, 5 to 7 minutes per side.

4. Transfer the brisket to a platter and pour away the excess fat from the pot.

5. Combine the remaining 3 tablespoons of oil with the garlic in a small bowl, and when brisket is cool enough to touch, rub the garlic mixture over the brisket, top and bottom.

6. Put half of the onions in the bottom of the pot and place the brisket on top.

7. Combine all the remaining ingredients, except the remaining onions and the stock, in a medium bowl. Mix well and spoon over the top of the brisket, then top with the onions.

8. Pour the stock around the outside of brisket, cover with a lid or very tightly with foil, and bake for 4 to 5 hours, until fork-tender (start checking after about 3 ½ hours). Oh, and don't be shocked by how much it shrinks.

9. Transfer to a cutting board, cover loosely with foil, and let rest for about 20 minutes before slicing.

10. Slice across the grain to serve—always across the grain (this is true for any protein), as that will shorten up the fibers and make it more tender to eat.

BRISKET FRIES WITH SPICY CHEESE SAUCE

MBOWYG (MEASUREMENTS BASED ON WHAT YOU'VE GOT)

5 MINUTES

You've undoubtedly heard of carne asada fries, right? Well, these are their way cooler cousin. And you can say what you want about processed cheese sauce—"It's not real cheese," "It's made with plastic," "That shit'll kill you"; it won't bother me cuz I've heard it and none of it matters. Because I don't know many things that go from nothing to hugely delicious in only a couple of minutes. And since this is a recipe based on any amount you might have, these will be easy, general instructions.

⅓ cup processed cheese sauce, such as Cheez Whiz

¼ teaspoon smoked paprika

¼ teaspoon chile powder

Pinch of kosher salt

1 big old handful leftover Jewish-Style Brisket (page 38), chopped into bite-size pieces

1 big old handful of cooked, crispy fries (about 1½ cups)

1. Put the processed cheese sauce in a small, microwave-safe bowl and add the paprika, chile powder, and salt.

2. Microwave on HIGH for about 30 seconds.

3. Stir to mix well, then heat again. Continue the process until it is hot enough to pour.

4. Microwave the brisket on HIGH 30 to 45 seconds, or until warm.

5. Plate the fries, top with brisket, and drizzle the sauce over the top.

WORLD'S BEST GRILLED CHEESE

You probably think I'm exaggerating; well, guess what—I'm not. You've already bought the book and my going over the top about this won't benefit me anymore. So go with your gut (literally and figuratively) and try this out.

2 tablespoons butter

1 garlic clove, finely minced

2 slices sourdough bread

1 to 2 tablespoons horseradish sauce (the mayo kind, not the grainy "prepared" kind)

1 tablespoon leftover Jewish-Style Brisket sauce (page 38)

2 slices Cheddar (white Cheddar, if possible)

3 to 4 ounces leftover Jewish-Style Brisket (page 38), warmed slightly

2 slices Monterey Jack

1. Put the butter and garlic in a small bowl and mix well.

2. Spread the horseradish sauce and brisket sauce on one slice of the bread. Add the Cheddar, then the heated brisket, then the Monterey Jack cheese, then top with second slice of bread.

3. Heat a nonstick skillet over medium-high heat.

4. Spread half the butter mixture on the top piece of the bread and cook, butter side down, until golden brown.

5. Spread the remaining butter mixture on what is now the top side, flip, and continue to cook until what is now the bottom is golden as well.

6. Eat—but not too quickly, even though you'll want to.

BRISKET EMPANADAS

Now we're having some fun! You could put anything in a pie dough crust and I'd eat it, and this is the perfect example.

One package (2 crusts) store-bought piecrust

1 tablespoon oil

½ yellow onion, diced

1 garlic clove, minced

2 cups chopped leftover Jewish-Style Brisket (page 38)

⅓ cup shredded Monterey Jack

⅓ cup finely chopped green onion

Kosher salt and freshly ground black pepper

4 teaspoons prepared horseradish

1 large egg yolk

About 1 tablespoon water

1. Preheat the oven to 350°F. Line a baking sheet with parchment.

2. Roll out each crust to be approximately 1 inch larger in diameter, then cut out five 5-inch circles with a bowl, cup, whatever. Squish up the remaining dough and roll it out again and make five more 5-inch circles from each crust.

3. Cook the onion in the oil in a skillet over medium heat until softened, about 3 minutes. Then add the garlic and cook for another minute.

4. Transfer the onion mixture to a bowl and let cool, then add the brisket, cheese, and green onion. Season with salt and pepper to taste and mix well to combine.

5. Put about ½ teaspoon of the horseradish in the center of each dough circle and spread it out, keeping it well away from the edges.

6. Put some of the brisket mixture in the middle of each circle. Dip your finger in water and wet the outer edge.

7. Fold each circle in half, being careful to keep the filling away from the edges. Crimp the edges with a fork to seal well, then place on the prepared baking sheet.

8. Whisk the egg yolk with the water and brush over the tops, then pierce the top of each empanada with two or three little holes to let steam escape.

9. Bake for 20 minutes, or until golden brown.

JUST ONE GREAT SIMPLE CHILI, AND THEN . . . .

This is one of those chapters where you could go to the store and simply grab the main item— in this case, canned chili— and get cooking. Would I prefer you make your own chili? Of course, because it will not only taste better, but you'll also be learning along the way, and that's a good thing.

Simple Chili
Appetizer Chili Fritos Bags
Chili Cornbread
Chili Shakshuka (Baked Eggs)
The Classic Chili Cheese Omelet

SIMPLE CHILI

Made even simpler because you are using the already cooked short ribs or brisket. Boo-ya!

2 tablespoons oil

½ small onion, diced

1 medium green bell pepper, seeded and diced

1 garlic clove, minced

One 15-ounce can whole peeled tomatoes

One 15-ounce can black beans, drained and rinsed

2 ounces canned, diced green chiles, chopped

3 tablespoons tomato paste

1 cup beef stock

1 teaspoon ground cumin

½ to 1 teaspoon chipotle chile powder

1 teaspoon kosher salt

½ teaspoon freshly ground black pepper

8 ounces leftover shredded Beer-Braised Short Ribs (page 28) or Jewish-Style Brisket (page 38)

½ cup leftover gravy/broth from Beer-Braised Short Ribs (page 28)

SUGGESTED TOPPINGS:

Something crunchy—from potato or tortilla chips to chopped red, white, or green onions

Chopped fresh cilantro

Lime wedges

Sour cream

Cheese

Diced avocado

Sliced jalapeño peppers

1. Heat the oil in a large pot over medium heat and add the onion and bell pepper. Cook until softened, about 5 minutes, then add the garlic and cook for another minute.

2. Add the tomatoes, breaking them up by hand before putting them in, then add everything else, except the short ribs and their broth, and cook over low heat for 20 minutes, stirring occasionally. Add the short ribs and broth, and cook until heated through.

3. Serve with the toppings as desired.

APPETIZER CHILI FRITOS BAGS

The dumbest but smartest recipe in the book—get it? Dumb because, well, wait until you see it. And smart because it is so compact, portable, and way, way good . . . if any of that makes sense.

Leftover Simple Chili (page 48), warmed up

One 1-ounce Fritos bag per appetizer

Suggested toppings: diced white onion, sour cream, jalapeño peppers, shredded cheese, hot sauce

1. Open each bag at the top.
2. Spoon in some chili.
3. Add any or all toppings that you'd like.
4. And now either:
   - Simply eat the chili with a fork or spoon
     OR
   - Close the top of the bag and shake really well to mix everything together. That sounds great in theory, but when I do it, I always end up wearing more of the chili than I eat. But I'll leave that up to you.

CHILI CORNBREAD

MAKES ONE 8-INCH SQUARE
PAN CORNBREAD

45 MINUTES

Supercheat alert cuz I'm using a cornbread mix—but who gives a shit when it's this good? And by the way, repurposing this cornbread into the bottom of an eggs Benedict is something that absolutely should be done.

One 11- to 15-ounce package cornbread mix for an 8-inch square pan

1 cup leftover Simple Chili (page 48)

⅓ cup diced green onion—this is a good place to use up the dark green stems

Butter, at room temperature, for topping

1. Grease an 8-inch square baking pan.

2. Empty the cornbread mix in a large bowl, then add two-thirds of the recommended water or milk plus the chili and green onions.

3. Mix well, transfer to the prepared baking pan, and bake as directed on the package.

4. And I'm not condoning this next move, but spreading slices of it with soft butter when you eat it wouldn't be the worst idea you've ever had.

CHILI SHAKSHUKA
(BAKED EGGS)

MAKES 1 SERVING, BUT CAN
EASILY BE DOUBLED OR
TRIPLED

25 MINUTES

Shakshuka is a spicy tomato and pepper sauce combo that's baked with eggs on top. It could easily win "most popular breakfast" anywhere in Israel. And while die-hard shakshuka fans will be mortified I'm using chili as my base, my chili also has tomatoes and peppers . . . so it's a natural stand-in, no?

About 1½ cups leftover Simple Chili (page 48) per person
1 or 2 large eggs per person
Kosher salt and freshly ground black pepper
Diced green onion for garnish

1. Preheat the oven to 375°F.

2. Put the chili in a small, ovenproof skillet and warm on the stove over medium heat, until just simmering. Note: You can't use a huge pan for a small amount of the chili because it will be spread too thin and the egg(s) will not cook properly. Try to have the chili be at least ½ inch thick in the pan.

3. Gently crack the eggs* on top of the chili and season with salt and pepper, then put the pan into the oven. Bake until the eggs are set to your liking, 8 to 12 minutes.

4. Garnish with green onion.

*If you hate runny yolks and don't want them here (which you should, btw), feel free to make scrambled eggs to go on top instead.

THE CLASSIC CHILI CHEESE OMELET

MAKES 1 OMELET

10 MINUTES

Raise your right hand and repeat after me:

"I [state your name] promise to learn how to make a proper omelet, and even if it becomes a horror show and turns into scrambled eggs, I will not give up and will keep trying until I get it right, so help me God."

Now we can begin.

2 large eggs

Kosher salt and freshly ground black pepper

1 tablespoon butter

¼ cup leftover Simple Chili (page 48), warmed

1 slice American cheese or 2 tablespoons of any shredded cheese you like—though I'd stay away from a straight Cheddar because I think it tends to dry out eggs.

1. Crack the eggs into a small bowl, add a pinch of salt and pepper, and beat with a fork until blended.

2. Melt the butter in a skillet over medium-high heat, making sure you coat the pan's bottom and sides well.

3. Pour in the beaten eggs and swirl to evenly coat the bottom of the pan.

4. Using a flexible spatula, slowly pull the setting egg in at the edges, just a little, to allow the unset egg to run in behind.

5. Continue to cook, gently swirling and tilting the pan if necessary, to create an evenly cooked surface.

6. When there is almost no uncooked egg left, add the chili to one-half of the omelet and immediately add the cheese.

7. Put your spatula under the edge of the omelet that has no chili on it and very gently, but in one swift motion, lift that side up to cover the chili and cheese.

8. Let it sit a minute or so to allow the cheese to melt, then carefully transfer to a plate.

9. And . . . how'd we do?

A DAMN GOOD MEATLOAF, AND THEN . . .

Is there anything better than a delicious meatloaf, hot out of the oven, on a plate with mashed potatoes? Hell yes, there is, and it's this completely changed version that's still crazy delicious . . . and then transforms into a bunch of other great stuff.

My Favorite Meatloaf
Gnocchi à la Delicious
Meatloaf Sloppys
Grilled Meatloaf Sandwich
Meat(loaf) Pasta Sauce
Meatloaf Tacos

MY FAVORITE MEATLOAF

MAKES ONE 2-POUND MEATLOAF

60 MINUTES

This will not just make you very happy, but will put an end to the "meatloaf again?" whining.

MEATLOAF:

1 pound ground beef

1 pound ground pork

1 pound frozen chopped spinach, thawed and squeezed dry

¾ cup panko bread crumbs

One 1-ounce package fajita seasoning

4 ounces canned diced green chiles

2 large eggs, beaten

GLAZE:

1 cup ketchup

⅓ cup apricot jam

2 tablespoons finely chopped chipotle chile

1. Preheat the oven to 350°F. Grease a 9-by-5-inch loaf pan or baking sheet.

2. Form the meatloaf: Mix together all the meatloaf ingredients in a medium bowl and transfer to the prepared loaf pan, or shape into a loaf and place on the prepared baking sheet.

3. Prepare the glaze: Mix together all the glaze ingredients in a bowl and spread about three-quarters of it over the meatloaf. Reserve the remaining glaze.

4. Bake for 45 minutes to 1 hour, until 155° to 160°F inside.

5. Remove from the oven, allow to cool slightly, slice into 1-inch-thick pieces, and coat with the reserved glaze before serving.

GNOCCHI À LA DELICIOUS

SERVES 4 TO 6
20 MINUTES

One of the easiest and quickest things you can make are gnocchi—those lovely little pillows of potato wrapped in pasta that cook in about 5 minutes. And when you add leftover meatloaf to the sauce . . .

Olive oil

1 pound leftover My Favorite Meatloaf (page 60), crumbled

2 garlic cloves, crushed

1 cup heavy cream

One 8-ounce can tomato sauce

2 tablespoons chopped fresh basil

1 pound potato gnocchi

Kosher salt and freshly ground black pepper

Chopped fresh parsley for garnish

1. Heat a large skillet over medium heat and add the oil. When it's hot, add the meatloaf and garlic. Stir to combine and heat through.

2. Once the meatloaf is warm, add the cream, tomato sauce, and basil. Stir and allow to thicken, about 5 minutes.

3. Meanwhile, boil the gnocchi in a large pot of water—when they float, they're ready.

4. Drain the gnocchi quickly and add to the sauce. Stir, season with salt and pepper to taste, and serve garnished with parsley.

MEATLOAF SLOPPYS

MAKES 6 SLOPPY JOES
20 MINUTES

Ahhhh yes, the amazing sloppy joe—what's not to like? Especially one made with chipotle (and leftover meatloaf). You'll notice this recipe calls for "good dark beer." If you wouldn't drink it, don't cook with it. Go for something with a little character. At the risk of being accused of pimping family, my cousin Peter owns the legendary San Diego brewery Alesmith—and his Speedway Stout, with its coffee notes, would be ideal. Failing that, use any stout or dark beer and you'll be happy.

1 tablespoon oil

½ onion, diced small

1 green bell pepper, seeded and diced small

1 large garlic clove, minced

1 pound leftover My Favorite Meatloaf (page 60), finely crumbled

2 tablespoons Worcestershire sauce

½ teaspoon kosher salt

6 ounces tomato paste

1 cup good dark beer

2 chipotle chiles, well minced

6 Hawaiian rolls, lightly toasted

½ cup crispy fried onions

1. Heat a large skillet over medium heat and add the oil. When it's hot, add the onion, bell pepper, and garlic. Cook until softened, about 5 minutes.

2. Add the crumbled meatloaf, Worcestershire, and salt, and mix really well to combine.

3. Then stir in the tomato paste, beer, and chipotle chiles. Continue to stir until all is beautifully blended and heated through.

4. Serve on Hawaiian rolls and top with the crispy onions.

GRILLED MEATLOAF SANDWICH

MAKES 2 FRICKING GREAT SANDWICHES

10 MINUTES (AND WORTH EVERY MINUTE)

Say what you want, but this is what meatloaf was really meant to be. There really is nuthin' better.

Enough ¾-inch-thick slices of leftover My Favorite Meatloaf (page 60) to cover 2 slices of bread

4 slices Muenster, provolone, or Havarti cheese

4 slices of a really good bread, such as sourdough, a hearty rye, whatever

¼ cup leftover My Favorite Meatloaf glaze (page 60)

2 tablespoons mayonnaise

Arugula for serving

1. Cook the meatloaf slices on a grill or nonstick skillet over medium-high heat until heated through and starting to get crispy.

2. When you flip the slices, add the cheese to the top.

3. Toast or grill the bread.

4. Mix together the glaze and mayo in a small bowl and spread on two slices of the toast.

5. To each sandwich base, add arugula, half of the cheese-topped meatloaf, and the final slice of bread.

MEAT(LOAF) PASTA SAUCE

One of the biggest pains when making a delicious meat sauce is messing with the meat. Well, guess what: with this version, the meat's already been messed with, and it's a snap!

2 tablespoons oil

1 small onion, diced

2 garlic cloves

2 cups crumbled leftover My Favorite Meatloaf (page 60)

One 28-ounce can whole, peeled tomatoes

1 tablespoon sugar

1 tablespoon Worcestershire sauce

1 teaspoon dried oregano

1. Heat the oil in a large skillet over medium heat, and when hot, add the onion. Cook until softened, about 3 minutes.

2. Add the garlic and cook until fragrant, about a minute.

3. Add the meatloaf and stir well to combine.

4. Squish the tomatoes into the pan by hand, breaking them up well. Add any extra can juices along with sugar, Worcestershire, and oregano.

5. Bring to a boil, then lower the heat and let simmer for 15 to 20 minutes.

6. It's so good.

MEATLOAF TACOS

Makes as many as you want, which could be a lot. This is just like we make at my restaurant—Not Not Tacos—and it's a damn popular taco.

FOR EACH TACO:

2 ounces leftover My Favorite
    Meatloaf (page 60)

Monterey Jack, shredded

1 small flour or corn tortilla

2 teaspoons sour cream

Iceberg lettuce, shredded

2 teaspoons leftover My Favorite
    Meatloaf sauce (page 60)

Crispy fried onions

Finely chopped green
    onion for garnish

1. Heat the meatloaf: A grill is nice; a nonstick skillet is, too; and frankly even a microwave on HIGH for 20 seconds or so is cool—the key is simply to heat it up. And when you turn it over to the second side, add the cheese so it can start melting.

2. Heat the tortilla—a nonstick skillet is perfect for this. You want it to start getting a little bit of color and become softer, that's all.

3. Then add the sour cream, lettuce, and the meatloaf with the cheese, and finally top with the crispy onions and green onion.

A BIG-ASS PERFECTLY COOKED STEAK, AND THEN . . .

You don't need a recipe on how
to cook a thin little steak;
just throw it on something hot
for a couple of minutes and
it'll be fine. But a good, thick,
beautifully marbled steak,
such as a rib eye, deserves
perfect cooking.

The Reverse Sear

The Best Leftover Steak Salad

Steak & Horseradish Crostini

Thai Beef Stir-Fry

Steak & Caramelized Onion Flatbread

THE REVERSE SEAR

There are many ways to cook a steak, and this is just one of them. But honestly, it might just be the best one, too. Because the goal for a steak to have a pink center is, frankly, for underachievers. The goal should be all pink—top to bottom, side to side, and end to end. And by simply following this method, that's exactly what you'll get, and you'll soon become the envy of your neighborhood. If you don't want that, simply keep quiet about it and don't show off to anyone.

You will definitely want a good instant-read digital thermometer, though.* It's nearly as important as the steak. It doesn't have to be expensive; it just has to be fast and accurate.

1 good steak, at least 1½ inches thick

Oil

Kosher salt and freshly ground black pepper

2 or 3 round slices any color onion, peeled and cut about ⅓ inch thick

*I used to gauge the doneness of a steak by pressing on different parts of my palm: the fat pad below my thumb— medium rare; the center of my palm—well done. I don't do that anymore because it never really worked. But what does work is an instant-read digital thermometer. You can get one for about $25, and it'll be one of the best gear purchases you'll make.

1. Preheat the oven to 275°F.

2. Lightly oil the steak and season liberally with salt and pepper on both sides.

3. Put the onion slices on a baking sheet, put steak on top, and place in the oven. Cook until somewhere between 125° and 135°F-ish. This part requires some discussion for two reasons: The first is that how rare or well done you like your steak is a very personal thing. I like a steak just slightly at medium rare, which is around 130°F for me—so it might take a try or two for you to nail your perfect temperature. But whatever that is, the steak will be that all the way through. The second thing is that you hear about resting time—the time after cooking a steak when it continues to rise in temperature. And that's exactly what happens when you've cooked a steak at a high temperature, such as on a grill or cast-iron skillet. But because we're cooking this slow, there's almost no rise in temperature once it's out of the oven.

4. The low-ish temperature of the oven has perfectly cooked your steak on the inside, but it definitely needs a little love on the outside, so start heating a cast-iron skillet, grill, grill pan, griddle, or whatever you have.

5. Put the steak on whatever hot surface you have and let it sear for no more than 30 to 45 seconds per side for a gorgeous color.

6. Then simply remove fit rom the surface, get out a sharp knife, and cut the steak (against the grain) to see your work.

7. And then take a pic to show your neighbors.

THE BEST LEFTOVER STEAK SALAD

SERVES 3—MAYBE 4,
BUT PROBABLY 3. YEAH,
3 SEEMS RIGHT.

15 MINUTES

This is at least a once-a-week item in our house.

1 cup nonfat Greek yogurt
  or sour cream

2 garlic cloves, minced

2 tablespoons fish sauce,*
  or about 1 tablespoon
  anchovy paste

1 tablespoon fresh lemon juice

1 tablespoon
  Worcestershire sauce

1 to 2 tablespoons milk

¼ cup fresh cilantro, chopped

Kosher salt

6 cups romaine lettuce,
  cut into small bites

8 ounces bacon, cooked until
  crispy and then crumbled

One 15-ounce can corn kernels,
  drained and cooked in a little
  oil until just starting to brown

12 to 16 ounces leftover Reverse
  Sear (page 74), thinly sliced

Freshly ground black pepper

1. Combine the yogurt, garlic, fish sauce, lemon juice, Worcestershire, milk, and cilantro in a small bowl. Mix until smooth and season to taste with salt.

2. Put the romaine in a large bowl and add the bacon, corn, and dressing. Toss well, then plate with the steak on top.

3. Add pepper to taste and serve.

*Don't freak out about fish sauce—it's not creepy, weird, or gross. It simply adds an amazing level of savoriness that makes everything better—and not in a fishy way. And btw, fish sauce is made from anchovies and you can use either, but pouring in a little fish sauce is infinitely easier than squishing up anchovy fillets.

STEAK & HORSERADISH CROSTINI

This is one of our favorite appetizers. But it's even more brilliant after a little late-night drinking or whatever, when you're stone-cold hungry. Get me?

This is simple. You'll broil a sliced baguette to give it a little color, spread on some horseradish sauce, add the steak, top with a little dressed arugula, and Bob's you're uncle. That's just a stupid old expression that generally means "and there you have it." But in my case, "Bob" was actually my uncle . . . so there.

HORSERADISH SAUCE:
¼ cup mayonnaise
¼ cup sour cream
2 to 3 tablespoons prepared white horseradish
1 tablespoon chopped fresh curly parsley
Kosher salt and freshly ground black pepper

CROSTINI:
Baby arugula
Olive oil
Sourdough baguette (or French, but sourdough is more interesting)
Leftover Reverse Sear (page 74)
Freshly ground black pepper (optional)

Make the horseradish sauce:
Combine all the sauce ingredients in a small bowl and set aside.

Make the crostini:
1. Put the arugula in a bowl, drizzle very lightly with olive oil, mix, and set aside.
2. Preheat the broiler.
3. Slice baguette lengthwise, drizzle lightly with olive oil, and put under the broiler until starting to get a little crispy, then remove.
4. Spread cut sides of the baguette with horseradish sauce, then add a layer of the arugula and top with sliced steak.
5. I like to give the top a final teeny drizzle of olive oil and a grind or two of pepper.
6. Cut baguette into smaller pieces and serve.

THAI BEEF STIR-FRY

MAKES 4 SERVINGS
15 MINUTES

Who says you can't use already-cooked steak for a stir-fry? Okay, probably a lot of people, but that's just BS cuz I do it all the time, and it works brilliantly.

2 tablespoons soy sauce

1 tablespoon fish sauce

1 teaspoon sugar

Juice of 1 lime

2 teaspoons oil

½ red bell pepper, seeded and thinly sliced

½ medium onion, thinly sliced

4 garlic cloves, minced

3 tablespoons peeled and minced fresh ginger

12 ounces leftover Reverse Sear (page 74), thinly sliced

1 cup fresh basil leaves, torn if large

3 cups Perfectly Steamed Rice (page 218) for serving

Fresh cilantro for garnish

1. Mix together the soy sauce, fish sauce, sugar, and lime juice in a small bowl until the sugar dissolves. Set aside.

2. Heat the oil in a wok or large skillet over high heat until almost smoking, then add the bell pepper, onion, garlic, and ginger, and stir-fry for a couple of minutes.

3. Add the beef, stir-fry about 30 seconds, then add the soy sauce mixture and stir to mix through, about 15 seconds. Then add the basil and cook until just wilted, maybe another 30 seconds.

4. Serve on the rice and garnish with cilantro.

STEAK & CARAMELIZED ONION FLATBREAD

Blue cheese and caramelized onions are one of the greatest food combos ever. Not to mention an especially great appetizer for when you are entertaining. This is the time for a very good red wine, btw.

1 tablespoon butter

1 teaspoon oil

1 medium red onion, thinly sliced

1 tablespoon brown sugar

⅓ cup balsamic vinegar

2 flatbreads, each about 8 inches in diameter

8 ounces leftover Reverse Sear (page 74)

4 ounces blue cheese, crumbled

1. Melt the butter and oil in a nonstick skillet over medium heat, then add the red onion. Cook for 5 minutes, or until really softened, then add the brown sugar and cook for 3 minutes more. Transfer to a bowl and wipe the pan clean.

2. Bring the balsamic vinegar to a simmer in small pot over medium-low heat, lower the heat to low, and let reduce until the consistency of maple syrup.

3. Preheat the broiler.

4. In the clean nonstick pan, heat each flatbread over medium-high heat for about 1 minute per side, just to soften, then put on a baking sheet.

5. Build: flatbread, generous layer of the onion mixture, some steak, and then blue cheese.

6. Broil on HIGH about a minute.

7. Evenly drizzle with some of the balsamic, cut, and eat.

KALUA PORK, AND THEN . . .

The more famous version of this
is a smoked pork shoulder, or
pork butt (which, btw, is not a
pig's butt at all). It's delicious
but can take up to 16 hours to
make. This Hawaiian version is
as delicious and takes less than
a third of the time in the oven,
which makes it accessible to
almost everyone. And then you get
to make this cool stuff:

Kalua Pork
Addictive Morning Hash
Kalua Pork Sliders
Kalua Pork Benedict
Chilaquiles

KALUA PORK

PROBABLY SERVES 10
4½ TO 5 HOURS

A favorite all over the Hawaiian Islands, and the crazy thing is I'm writing out this recipe sitting on a balcony in Maui—and no, why would I make that up? Just see the pic.

One 5-pound pork butt or shoulder (it's the same thing)

10 garlic cloves, peeled and cut in half lengthwise

2 to 3 tablespoons liquid smoke

2 tablespoons Hawaiian alaea salt or kosher salt

1. Preheat the oven to 325°F.

2. Using a paring knife, make twenty 1-inch slits all around the pork and insert a garlic clove half into each slit.

3. Rub pork with the liquid smoke and apply salt evenly.

4. Double-wrap tightly in foil, place on a baking sheet, and bake for 4½ to 5 hours, until very tender and shreddable.

5. Serve every way you can think of: in a sandwich with crispy cabbage, as a taco, the filling for a cheesy quesadilla, or in place of the ham on a Benedict—they're all good.

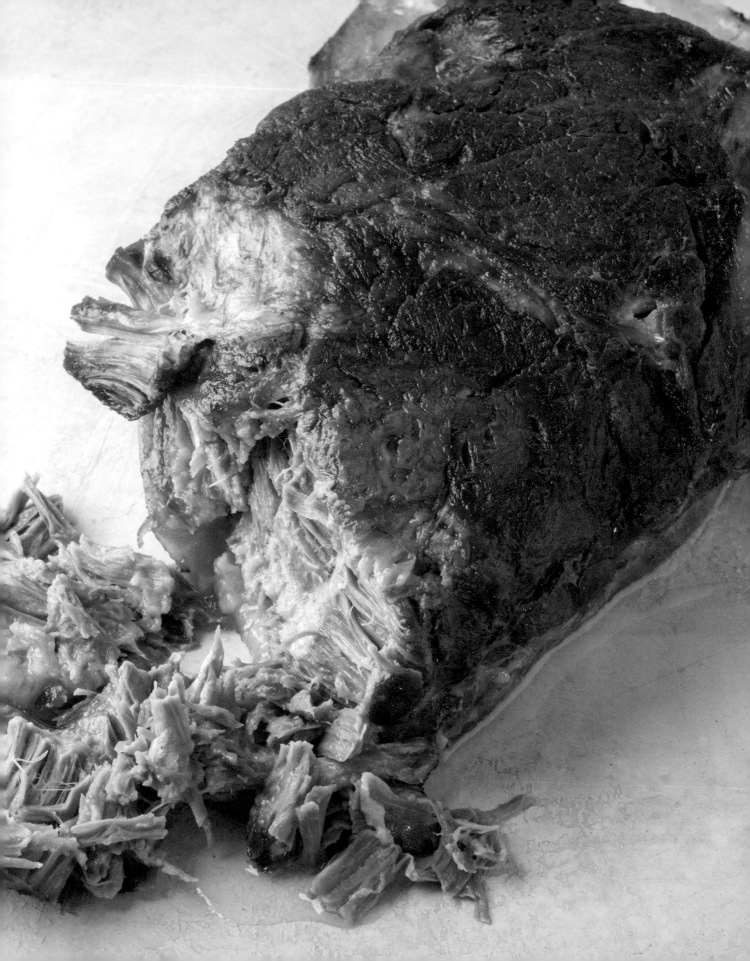

ADDICTIVE MORNING HASH

SERVES 2
15 MINUTES

Ah, yes, hash, the "cleanup batter" of the breakfast game. Anything can go into hash—leftover chicken, bacon, lasagna, chopped up tamales—anything. But when you have a little pile of leftover kalua pork . . . it's like you've won the fricking breakfast lottery.

2 tablespoons butter

2 tablespoons avocado oil

⅓ cup seeded and diced red bell pepper

½ cup diced red onion

8 ounces leftover fries, diced, such as Ridiculously Good Fries (page 192); you could even use leftover tots!

1 garlic clove, minced

6 ounces leftover Kalua Pork (page 86)

4 large eggs: poached, fried, scrambled, it's up to you— okay, no, it's not because a hash needs a runny yolk, so poach or fry 'em

1. Heat the butter and oil in a large nonstick skillet over medium heat.

2. When the butter has melted, spread it and the oil around evenly. Add the bell pepper and onion to one side of the pan, and the fries to the other.

3. You have two goals here: to cook the onion and pepper until just softened, and to get the fries crispyish. When you're there, 3 to 5 minutes, add the garlic and mix a bit. When it's fragrant, about 45 seconds, put in the pork and mix everything well to combine.

4. At this point, I like to flatten the whole thing out and let it get crispy on the bottom.

5. When it is done, I like to serve it, crispy side up, with the eggs on top.

KALUA PORK SLIDERS

MBOWYG

15 MINUTES

This is the obvious leftover move when it comes to any kind of shredded pork product. A bun, some pork, maybe a little BBQ sauce, and you're there. But we can do better than that, right? Right. So here are some choices to change shit up a bit . . .

Leftover Kalua Pork (page 86)—hard to say how much cuz I don't know what bread you're using

THE BREAD:

Hawaiian roll—the classic choice

Brioche bun—sweet like the Hawaiian but a bit more upmarket

Baguette—not normally used, but a good sourdough one is genius, and, cut into 2-inch pieces, it's quite sliderlike

English muffin—why the hell not

Any slider roll—yup, they work all day long

THE SAUCE—IT ALWAYS NEEDS A LITTLE, AND ANY OF THESE WILL DO FINE:

BBQ—the classic

Hoisin—a kind of Chinese BBQ sauce and my favorite here when mixed with a little mayo

Mustard mayo—I go about 60/40 mustard to mayo, and it's a really nice, not-sweet option

Fry sauce (page 195)—is supergood on these

THE VEGGIES:

Coleslaw—don't feel obligated to make your own; even the bagged kind that comes with its own sauce from the store is a great sub

Crispy shredded iceberg lettuce—works perfectly

Fancy Bibb lettuce, etc.—hell no

Pickles—yes

Pickled jalapeño peppers—double yes!

Grilled pineapple—if you wanna go full Hawaiian, then this your move. Simply brush slices of pineapple with a little oil and throw on the grill. Let them get really good grill marks on each side before removing. Then either dice or use slices whole on the slider.

THE CRUNCH—CRUNCH IS KEY:

Crispy fried onions—the kind you use at Thanksgiving are very good

Potato chips—another of my faves (especially Maui onion flavor, if you can find them)

The build:

1. Heat up the pork—10 or 15 seconds in a microwave on HIGH should do it.

2. Toast whatever bread you're using a little, and don't argue cuz this step is important.

3. Add the sauce to the bottom half of the bread.

4. Add the veggies.

5. Add the heated-up Kalua pork.

6. Add the crunch.

7. Add a little more sauce and the top half of the bread.

KALUA PORK BENEDICT

I believe my final meal (if I have any say in it) will be some type of Benedict. There's just something about them that makes me insanely happy . . . especially the way the rich, delicious yolk runs down the side and makes everything better. And this one is no exception.

4 English muffins

Butter

½ cup Pickled Red Onions (recipe follows)

1 generous cup leftover Kalua Pork (page 86), heated up

4 Poached Eggs (page 126)

1 cup Blender Hollandaise (recipe follows)

1. Toast, then butter the English muffins.

2. Top each with pickled onions, ¼ cup of pork, a poached egg, and finally ¼ cup of hollandaise.

(continues)

PICKLED RED ONIONS

**MAKES ABOUT 1½ CUPS
PICKLED ONIONS**

**AT LEAST 2 HOURS, BUT
BETTER OVERNIGHT**

½ cup cider vinegar

1 cup water

1½ teaspoons kosher salt

6 to 10 black peppercorns

2 tablespoons sugar

1 medium red onion, sliced
  into thin semicircles

1. Combine everything except the onion in a small bowl and stir well to dissolve the sugar and salt.

2. Put the sliced onion in a large bowl and cover with boiling water. Let sit for about a minute, then drain well.

3. When the onion is cool enough to handle, put as many slices as you can into a sterilized pint-size mason jar and cover with the brine liquid.

4. Let cool, screw on the lid, and refrigerate.

5. Give 'em at least a couple of hours, but they'll start getting really good tomorrow, and they'll be great after 2 days or so.

BLENDER HOLLANDAISE

**MAKES ABOUT 1¼ CUPS
HOLLANDAISE**

5 MINUTES

10 tablespoons butter

3 large egg yolks

1 tablespoon fresh lemon juice

⅛ teaspoon cayenne pepper

Pinch of kosher salt

1. Melt butter in a small pot over low heat—don't let it burn.

2. Combine egg yolks, lemon juice, cayenne, and salt in a blender. Blend on medium speed for about 30 seconds, or until very light yellow in color.

3. Reduce the blender speed to low and slowly drizzle in melted butter.

4. Blend until everything is mixed and thickened nicely.

5. Turn off the blender, taste, and use.

CHILAQUILES

One of my favorite breakfasts, chilaquiles ("chee-lah-kee-les") are essentially tortillas that have been cut, fried in oil, simmered in red or green salsa to soften, and served with cheese, shredded chicken, roasted veggies, etc., then topped with a scrambled or fried egg. But all that is a complete hassle to me, so I shortcut it with store-bought tortilla chips, and it's still amazing (especially when served with leftover Kalua pork). Best. Thing. Ever.

⅔ cup green enchilada sauce

Tortilla chips

2 cups leftover Kalua Pork (page 86)

⅔ cup salsa verde (green salsa)

1½ cups shredded Monterey Jack

4 large eggs

Fresh cilantro for garnish

1. Cover the bottom of a Pyrex pie plate with half of the enchilada sauce.

2. Cover the sauce completely with a layer of tortilla chips.

3. Top that with half of the pork, half of the salsa, and then half of the cheese.

4. Top with more enchilada sauce, more chips, more pork, and more salsa, then finish with the remaining cheese.

5. Microwave on HIGH for 5 minutes.

6. While it cooks, make your eggs—fried would be great but whatever works for you, then put them on the now done chilaquiles and garnish with cilantro.

7. Eat.

THE PERFECT ROAST CHICKEN, AND THEN . . .

Honestly, this chapter could be a whole book by itself cuz a chicken is one of those things that can become almost anything: a soup, a salad, a pie, a pizza (okay, a braided one, actually) . . . but really just whatever. It's just your starting point for a world of deliciousness—so grab the ring and get effing going! Here, chick chick chick . . .

The Perfect Roast Chicken

Braided Buffalo Chicken Pizza

Chicken Noodle Wonton Soup

Chimichitos

Thai Chicken Curry

Baked Chicken Taquitos

5-Minute Chicken Tortilla Soup

THE PERFECT ROAST CHICKEN

MAKES 1 CHICKEN (BUT A REALLY DAMN GOOD ONE)

3½ HOURS

I've always thought of chicken as the little black dress of the food world. It can be sophisticated for a Friday night or casual for a Sunday lunch. I actually started writing this book with a different chicken recipe in mind, but I started making this version a few months ago and can't stop. It's moist, it's tender—it's everything you want in a chicken. So whatever you do, just make one . . . or two.

One 3½- to 4-pound chicken; a little bigger is no problem

Kosher salt and freshly ground black pepper

1 lemon, quartered

1 garlic head, halved crosswise

2 to 3 tablespoons olive oil or 2 to 3 tablespoons butter, at room temperature

1. Preheat the oven to 300°F. Place a rack (if you have one, and you should) in a roasting pan large enough to hold the chicken.

2. Remove anything from inside the chicken (neck, giblets, etc.) and save for another use. Dry the chicken thoroughly with paper towels.*

3. Put chicken on the rack in the roasting pan.

4. Salt and pepper the inside of the chicken, then insert the lemon quarters and garlic head.

5. Rub outside of the chicken with oil or butter and season well with salt and pepper.

6. Tie the legs together with kitchen string (nothing fancy; you just want to keep them from going rogue during cooking) and tuck the wing tips under the body of the chicken.

7. Roast in the oven until the skin is nicely browned and the chicken is tender, about 3 hours, or until it reaches an internal temperature of 160°F.

8. Remove from the oven and let the chicken rest for 15 minutes before carving.

*There's no need to rinse or wash the chicken to remove bacteria. The fact that you're going to cook it will take care of that. The only thing washing a chicken will really do is to possibly splatter chicken grossness all over your sink and counter—and that's not necessarily a good thing. And if you don't want to believe me, perhaps the US Centers for Disease Control and Prevention can convince you: "During washing, chicken juices can spread in the kitchen and contaminate other foods, utensils, and countertops."

BRAIDED BUFFALO CHICKEN PIZZA

SERVES 4 TO 6

45 MINUTES

Pizza is generally flat and round, which is fine but can definitely get boring. This pizza is neither flat nor round; and once you get the hang of the braiding part, you'll realize you can do this with any pizza—and you should! Oh, and it's probably more of a braided calzone than a pizza . . . just saying.

1 ball pizza dough

1 ounce crumbled blue cheese

2 tablespoons mayonnaise

2 tablespoons sour cream

1 tablespoon milk

½ teaspoon Worcestershire sauce

Pinch of kosher salt, plus more for sprinkling

3 or 4 grinds black pepper, plus more for sprinkling

3 tablespoons butter

6 ounces hot sauce

2 cups shredded leftover Perfect Roast Chicken (page 100)

Cooking spray for pan (optional)

½ small red onion, slivered

¾ cup shredded mozzarella

Oil for brushing

1. Preheat the oven to 375°F and remove the dough from the fridge.

2. Combine the blue cheese, mayo, sour cream, milk, Worcestershire sauce, salt, and pepper in a bowl. Stir until well mixed, then set aside.

3. Microwave the butter and hot sauce together on HIGH in a medium microwave-safe bowl until the butter has melted, about 15 seconds. Then remove the bowl from the microwave and add chicken. Mix until well combined.

4. Spray a large baking sheet with cooking spray or line it with parchment paper.

5. Shape the dough into a 9-by-13-inch rectangle on the prepared baking sheet.

6. Spread the chicken in a 3-inch strip lengthwise down center of the dough, all the way to ends, and top with the blue cheese mixture, the red onion, and finally the cheese.

7. On both of the empty sides, make diagonal slices an inch apart from the edge of the filling to the dough edge.

8. Get braiding one over the other. Alternating from side to side, braid the strips of dough at a slight angle across the filling.

9. Brush lightly with oil, season generously with salt and pepper, and bake 20 to 25 minutes, or until golden brown.

10. Yum.

CHICKEN NOODLE WONTON SOUP

SERVES 4
20 MINUTES

A Jewish grandmother and a Chinese grandmother walk into a kitchen . . . and this happens. 男孩, 我曾经很开心 (and am I ever happy it did).

2 tablespoons oil

½ small onion, sliced

2 medium carrots, cut diagonally into thin slices

1 celery stalk, cut diagonally into thin slices

One 1-inch piece fresh ginger, thinly sliced

3 garlic cloves, crushed and roughly chopped

6 cups chicken stock

6 green onions, white and light green parts, cut into 1-inch pieces

8 frozen chicken or pork pot stickers

4 baby bok choy, root end cut off so leaves can separate, then sliced lengthwise

One 3-ounce package instant ramen noodles, seasoning pack removed

8 shiitake mushrooms, stemmed and thinly sliced

8 ounces leftover Perfect Roast Chicken (page 100)

1 tablespoon soy sauce

1 teaspoon sesame chili oil (or just sesame oil)

1. Heat the oil in a medium pot over medium heat. Add the onion, carrots, and celery and cook until softened, about 5 minutes.

2. Add the ginger and garlic and cook, stirring, until fragrant, about a minute.

3. Add the stock and green onions and bring to a simmer. Cook for 5 minutes.

4. Put in the pot stickers and cook for 5 minutes, then add the bok choy, noodles, shiitakes, and chicken.

5. Cook until the noodles are softened, about 5 minutes, then stir in the soy sauce and sesame chili oil.

6. Serve.

CHIMICHITOS

Think half chimichanga and half burrito. They're extra cool cuz they're baked, not fried—not that that's a bad thing . . .

3 cups shredded leftover Perfect Roast Chicken (page 100)

1 cup chunky red salsa

One 4-ounce can diced green chiles

4 burrito-size flour tortillas

1 tablespoon oil

1 cup red enchilada sauce

Sour cream for garnish

Shredded Cheddar cheese for garnish

Fresh cilantro for garnish

1. Preheat the oven to 400°F. Grease a baking sheet and set aside.

2. Combine the chicken, salsa, and chiles in a large bowl and mix well.

3. Heat the tortillas just a bit to make them a little more pliable—microwave or in a skillet on the stovetop is fine.

4. Spoon some of the chicken mixture onto each tortilla, then roll up like a cigar (or whatever is legal where you are), restaurant-style: edge nearest you over the filling, sides in, then roll away from you.

5. Place on the prepared baking sheet and brush the tops lightly with oil.

6. Bake until golden, 20 to 25 minutes.

7. While they cook, warm the enchilada sauce any way you want.

8. When they're done, spoon some warm enchilada sauce on a plate, lay a chimichito on top, add some sour cream, and sprinkle with cheese and cilantro.

THAI CHICKEN CURRY

My sister-in-law Cheryl sent this recipe to me years ago, and we fricking love it. Take my advice: when you go to buy the coconut milk for this, buy two cans because you'll want to make it again right after.

1 tablespoon oil

1 small onion, diced

1 garlic clove, crushed

1 tablespoon all-purpose flour

2 tablespoons curry powder

One 14-ounce can coconut milk

3 tablespoons apricot jam

1 tablespoon sriracha

2 cups shredded leftover
  Perfect Roast Chicken
  (page 100)

Chopped fresh cilantro
  for garnish

1. Heat the oil in a large nonstick skillet over medium heat and cook the onion and garlic until softened, but not too soft.

2. Mix together the flour and curry powder in a small bowl and add to the onion mixture. Stir for a couple of minutes—the onion mixture will become very dry.

3. Add the coconut milk, apricot jam, and sriracha and stir well for a couple of minutes, making sure you get what's on the bottom mixed in.

4. Add the chicken and let all the gorgeousness warm through.

5. Serve on rice, garnished with a little cilantro.

BAKED CHICKEN TAQUITOS

Just like at your favorite taco shop, but you bake them at home instead of buying them there. And that means you can make them in your jammies. Pretty nice, huh?

Cooking spray for pan

2 cups shredded leftover Perfect Roast Chicken (page 100)

⅓ cup green salsa

1 tablespoon finely minced chipotle chile

½ cup shredded Monterey Jack

12 small flour tortillas

For serving: sour cream, guacamole, salsa, queso fresco, limes, etc.

1. Preheat the oven to 425°F. Spray a baking sheet with cooking spray and set aside.

2. Combine the chicken, salsa, chipotle, and cheese in a large bowl and mix well.

3. Warm the tortillas in a nonstick skillet until just softened and pliable, about 15 seconds per side.

4. Add some of the chicken mixture to each tortilla, roll up tight, and place, seam side down, on the prepared baking sheet.

5. Spray tops lightly with oil and bake about 25 minutes, or until beginning to brown at the edges.

6. Serve with sour cream, guac, etc.

5-MINUTE CHICKEN TORTILLA SOUP

SERVES 4, I THINK
5 MINUTES

Even though this will likely offend Mexican grandmothers everywhere (because of the jarred red salsa cheat), it's so good and I eat it often.

16 ounces medium-hot red salsa

2 cups chicken stock

2 cups shredded leftover Perfect Roast Chicken (page 100)

2 flour tortillas

Oil

1 ripe avocado, peeled, pitted, and diced

2 tablespoons chopped fresh cilantro

1. Combine the salsa and stock in a large pot and simmer over medium heat until everything is heated through.

2. Meanwhile, rub each side of the tortillas very lightly with oil, then cook in a nonstick skillet over medium heat, flipping once, until just beginning to get a tiny bit browned and crispy on each side.

3. Slice each tortilla in half and then into thin strips.

4. To serve, put some soup in a bowl and top with avocado, tortilla strips, and cilantro.

THANKSGIVING, AND THEN . . . .

My friend Leigh calls
Thanksgiving the Super Bowl
of leftovers—and she's right.
Oh, sure, you could argue July
Fourth, and you'd be close . . .
but it doesn't come close in
variety. Not just because the
options are fricking endless but
because those options are also
fricking delicious. And while
this chapter isn't about making a
turkey, stuffing, and so on, it
is about what to do when you have
those left over.

Stuffing Omelet

Stuffing Balls

Turkey & Stuffing Tacos with
Cranberry Sour Cream

Hoisin Turkey Lettuce Cups

Turkey & Dumplings

Thanksgiving Benedict

Pumpkin Bourbon Shake

STUFFING OMELET

MAKES 1 OMELET
10 MINUTES

Don't you dare laugh until you've tried it. This has been a tradition in my house for nearly 25 years. And although it's in its natural habitat during Thanksgiving, it's so good we often buy a stovetop-style stuffing mix and have this in the summer.

2 large eggs

Kosher salt and freshly ground black pepper

1 tablespoon butter

3 tablespoons leftover stuffing, warmed in a microwave

1 slice American cheese—just go with me on this

1. Crack the eggs into a small bowl, add salt and pepper, and beat well.

2. Heat a small nonstick skillet over medium-high heat. Using a spatula, coat the bottom and sides thoroughly with the butter, then add the beaten eggs.

3. Swirl gently, allowing the eggs to begin to stick up the sides and to the bottom.

4. Using the spatula, gently pull the setting egg away from the sides, allowing the unset egg to run in behind. Your goal—if it isn't obvious—is to create a fairly uniform layer of egg across the bottom and a little up the sides of the pan.

5. Now add the stuffing across about half of the omelet. Tear the cheese in half and cover the stuffing.

6. Using the spatula, gently fold the half with no stuffing over the stuffing half.

7. Cook for another minute or so, then carefully flip over and cook for another minute—this will help the cheese melt.

8. Remove from the pan and serve—and wait for next Thanksgiving.

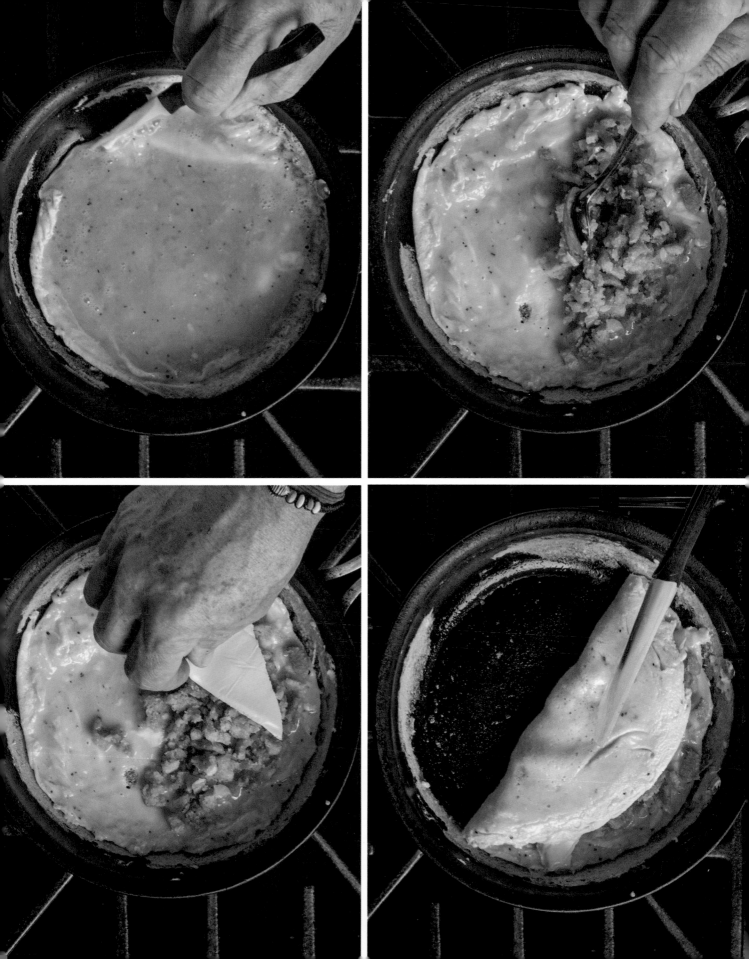

STUFFING BALLS

I know what you're thinking: "*I didn't even know stuffing had balls.*" Boy, am I funny, or not? And btw, that's the same stupid joke I've been using ever since I shot an episode in Hong Kong for my Discovery Channel series called *Just Cook This*. I was in the middle of a street food segment, eating fish balls (ground fish, spices, etc.), turned to the camera, and said, "*I didn't even know fish had balls.*" I thought it was funny, but some boring executive didn't, and the line got cut. Was that so bad? In any case, these little one-biters are so good—and always welcome.

And can there ever be enough stuffing?

2 large eggs, beaten

½ cup panko bread crumbs

⅓ cup finely grated Parmesan

Oil for hands

1 cup leftover stuffing, slightly warmed in a microwave

⅓ cup sour cream

1 to 2 tablespoons sriracha— I just don't know how spicy you like it

1. Preheat the oven to 400°F.

2. Put the eggs in one bowl and the panko and Parm in another.

3. Very lightly oil your hands.

4. Take about 1½ tablespoons of warmed stuffing and roll it into a tight little ball. Repeat until all the balls are formed.

5. Roll the balls through the beaten egg, then through the panko mixture, coating well, and place on an ungreased baking sheet.

6. Bake until golden and crispy, 20 to 25 minutes.

7. Combine the sour cream and sriracha in a small bowl. Mix well and serve alongside the balls.

TURKEY & STUFFING TACOS WITH CRANBERRY SOUR CREAM

I never reach for, or ever have, cranberry sauce on Thanksgiving. Ever. But the cranberry sour cream in this is so damn good.

¼ cup sour cream

1 tablespoon leftover cranberry sauce

Four 5-inch flour tortillas (corn would also work, I suppose—I'm just not a fan of them here)

8 ounces sliced leftover turkey

Oil for pan

1 cup leftover stuffing

⅓ cup crispy fried onions, the green bean casserole kind

1. Combine the sour cream and cranberry sauce in a small bowl and mix well.

2. Warm or cook the flour tortillas in a nonstick skillet.

3. Warm the turkey and stuffing. Note: Of course a microwave will do this just fine, but since you already have the nonstick pan out, I suggest you warm the turkey in that. Add a few drops of oil, and the turkey will not just warm up but will start to get crispy edges that will intensify the flavor—just a thought.

4. Build: tortilla, sour cream, turkey, stuffing and then the crispy onions.

5. Damn.

HOISIN TURKEY LETTUCE CUPS

MAKES 10 FILLED LETTUCE CUPS

15 MINUTES

This is an often requested dinner from my wife, Kelly, though it's more often made with the turkey's cousin—a chicken.

6 tablespoons hoisin sauce

1 tablespoon soy sauce

1 tablespoon sriracha

1½ teaspoons oil

⅓ cup seeded and small-diced red bell pepper

2 cups diced leftover turkey

10 Bibb lettuce cups, each roughly the size of a small hand

¼ cup finely diced green onion

About ¼ cup of something crunchy: crispy chow mein noodles are ideal; peanuts or cashews would work great, too—walnuts not so much, though

1. Combine the hoisin, soy sauce, and sriracha in a small bowl. Mix well and set aside.

2. Heat a wok or large skillet over medium heat. Add the oil and swirl it around.

3. Add the bell pepper and cook until softened, about 3 minutes.

4. Add the diced turkey and stir well to combine.

5. When the turkey mixture has been warmed through, add the hoisin mixture and stir quickly, making sure all is coated well.

6. Remove from the heat and divide among the lettuce cups. Top each with green onion and crunchies.

TURKEY & DUMPLINGS

Get ready to put on your grandma panties and make a bunch of people happy—wait, that didn't come out quite right. I just meant that, to me, this is very much something a grandma would cook, and because you'll be making it . . . oh, never mind.

2 tablespoons butter

1 onion, diced

2 carrots, diced small

2 celery stalks, including their leaves, diced

¼ cup all-purpose flour

4 cups turkey stock if you have it; if not, chicken stock will be just fine

2 cups shredded leftover turkey—diced is fine, too

½ cup milk

½ teaspoon dried thyme

½ teaspoon dried sage

½ teaspoon baking powder

Kosher salt and freshly ground black pepper

DUMPLINGS:

1 cup biscuit baking mix

⅓ cup 2% milk

1. Melt the butter in a large pot over medium heat and add the onion, carrots, and celery. Cook until softened, about 5 minutes.

2. Add the flour and stir for about a minute. The mixture will be a dry, sandy mess, but only for a sec.

3. Add the stock and stir well, scraping up what's stuck on the bottom, then bring to a boil.

4. Lower the heat to a simmer and add the turkey, milk, thyme, sage, and baking powder. Stir well and season to taste with salt and pepper.

5. Make the dumplings: Combine the baking mix and milk in a small bowl and mix until just moistened.

6. Add generous tablespoonfuls of the dumpling mix to the top of the simmering turkey mixture.

7. Cover the pot and cook over low heat for 20 to 25 minutes (without lifting the lid, please), until the dumplings are little pillows of deliciousness floating on top.

THANKSGIVING BENEDICT

MAKES 4 BENEDICTS
20 MINUTES

Crispy stuffing, hot turkey, and gravy? Hallelujah!

3 cups leftover stuffing
1 tablespoon oil
1 tablespoon butter
8 ounces leftover cooked turkey
4 poached large eggs
   (recipe follows)
¾ cup leftover turkey gravy
   (if stuck, go with chicken
   or even beef gravy)
Finely chopped fresh
   parsley for garnish

1. Shape the stuffing into four ½-inch-thick patties.

2. Heat a large nonstick skillet over medium-high heat, add the oil and butter, and when they melt, spread evenly over the bottom of the pan.

3. Place the patties in the pan and cook for about 4 minutes per side, or until getting crispy. Remove from the heat but keep warm.

4. Heat the turkey (a microwave is perfectly acceptable here).

5. To serve, put a stuffing patty on a plate, top with turkey and a poached egg, and finally add some gravy.

6. Garnish with parsley and serve.

POACHED EGGS

Once you get this down, you'll be poaching eggs all the damn time.

Egg(s)*
2 tablespoons white vinegar

*And btw, if not using right away, put the just-poached egg(s) into ice water. Once cooled down, poached eggs will keep for a couple of days in water in the fridge. When you want to use them, just bring a small pot of water to a simmer. Slip in the egg(s) for about a minute, then simply remove and use.

1. Pour at least 5 to 6 inches of water in a medium saucepan. Bring to just a simmer over medium-high heat—not boiling, but just before (180° to 190°F).

2. Add the vinegar and stir to mix—the vinegar will help pull the egg whites together.

3. Crack an egg into a small cup.

4. Using a large spoon, swirl the simmering water (to create a mini vortex), lower the cup with its egg almost to the top of the simmering, swirling water, then gently slip the egg out of the cup and into the center of the swirl—the egg white will slowly come together.

5. Using a slotted spoon, check the egg after about 3 minutes—the white should be set and the yolk soft.

6. Remove from the pot, let water drain off, and use. Cook any remaining eggs the same way, one at a time.

PUMPKIN BOURBON SHAKE

You can keep your grande Starbucks pumpkin-spiced latte with organic soy milk. Cuz when it comes to a pumpkin drink, this is the only one I want.

1 slice pumpkin pie
1 cup vanilla ice cream
½ cup milk
2 tablespoons bourbon, plus more to float (optional)
2 tablespoons chopped pecans

1. Put the pie, ice cream, milk, and bourbon in a blender.

2. Blend until your desired thickness is reached, adding more milk if you like it thinner.

3. Stop, add the pecans, give it one more quick blitz, and serve.

4. Fine, a float of a little more bourbon wouldn't be the worst thing you could do.

PERFECTLY HARD-BOILED EGGS, AND THEN . . .

Think this is a dumb category?
Think again cuz a well-executed
hard-boiled egg is art. But they
really shine when you do this
stuff with 'em . . .

Perfectly Hard-Boiled Eggs
Curried Egg Salad
Everything Egg Avotoast
Chorizo Scotch Eggs
Kalua Pork Deviled Eggs

PERFECTLY HARD-BOILED EGGS

MAKES AS MANY AS YOU WANT
15 MINUTES

I remember when I shot an egg episode for my TV show years ago; one of the segments was how to hard-boil an egg so you didn't get that gross, gray ring. Kelly said, "Isn't that kind of basic?" And I thought, "Well, when I learned how, it changed a lot for me." Because it's just not about the gray ring, but doing it wrong also dries out the yolk and makes it chalky tasting. But since then I've had a jillion people tell me they no longer eff up hard-boiled eggs because of this. So now I use Kelly as sort of a reverse predictor of recipe success: if she says, "That's a stupid recipe," it's almost guaranteed to be popular.

Eggs—as many as you need

1. Fill a big bowl with ice and water and set aside.

2. Carefully put the eggs in a medium saucepan and fill with cold water, covering them by about an inch—and I say carefully because even a tiny little crack can result in a grotesque "Elephant man"–style egg.

3. Over medium-high heat, bring the water to a rolling boil. As soon as it does, turn off the heat and cover the pot with a lid.

4. After 9 minutes, carefully pour the hot water from the pot and immediately put the eggs into the ice water bath—this will stop them from cooking further.

5. Then just use 'em. And btw, an egg has only about 70 calories, which makes it a perfect snack, especially when drizzled with a little hot sauce or mustard . . . or both.

CURRIED EGG SALAD

MAKES ABOUT 1½ CUPS
EGG SALAD

10 MINUTES

This is great right outta the fridge (my favorite way, I might add), or in a sandwich (toasted, of course), or on a cracker, or even on a bed of greens. At Not Not Tacos, for a while we had a curried egg salad taco that was my absolute fave. But in the shadow of other, more popular tacos, such as Korean short rib, cheeseburger, pastrami, and smoky pork and mac, it got no love and was pulled. But I still make it all the time.

6 leftover Perfectly Hard-Boiled Eggs (page 132), peeled

¼ cup diced green onion, white and light green parts

¼ cup finely diced celery

2 to 3 teaspoons curry powder

6 tablespoons mayo—this part can be tricky because some people like drier egg salad than others (not me), so maybe start with ¼ cup and go from there

Kosher salt and freshly ground black pepper

Grate or chop the eggs in a large bowl and add the green onion, celery, curry powder, mayo, and a pinch each of salt and pepper. Mix well.

EVERYTHING EGG AVOTOAST

The morning I wrote out this recipe, I just happened to have one. And it made me really happy I had the brilliance . . . I mean, the foresight . . . to put this recipe in the book.

1 large avocado, peeled
  and pitted

1 teaspoon fresh lemon juice

Kosher salt and freshly
  ground black pepper

3 thick slices whole-grain bread

2 leftover Perfectly Hard-Boiled
  Eggs (page 132), peeled

1 teaspoon light mayonnaise

½ teaspoon Dijon mustard

1 teaspoon everything
  bagel seasoning

1. Combine the avocado and lemon juice in a small bowl, using a fork to mash. Season to taste with salt and pepper.

2. Toast the bread.

3. Put the eggs in a small bowl, adding the mayo, Dijon, salt, and pepper. Use the back of a fork to mash and combine well.

4. Spread the mashed avocado on the toast. Top with the egg salad. Sprinkle with the everything bagel seasoning.

CHORIZO SCOTCH EGGS

MAKES 6 SCOTCH EGGS
45 MINUTES

My first Scotch egg was in a pub in London, and it was amazing. Okay, so maybe there was a little beer involved, but still. Anyway, they're hard-boiled eggs that are traditionally wrapped with sausage, rolled in bread crumbs, and deep-fried. But that's a full-on hassle, so we bake 'em instead. They rule.

1 pound pork chorizo, the Mexican kind, not the Spanish kind (and if you can't find that, any kind of uncooked sausage will do)
6 leftover Perfectly Hard-Boiled Eggs (page 132), peeled
1 cup all-purpose flour
2 large eggs, beaten
2 cups panko bread crumbs
Oil for deep-frying (optional)

1. Preheat the oven to 400°F.

2. Separate the chorizo into six balls, then flatten each into about a 5-inch circle.

3. Wrap each egg with a circle of chorizo, making sure there are no gaps.

4. Place the flour in a large bowl and coat each ball with flour, shaking off any excess.

5. Dip each flour-coated ball in the beaten egg and then coat well with the bread crumbs.

6. Put on a baking sheet and bake for 30 minutes, or until crispy and cooked through.

7. But if you want to deep-fry them: Heat about 3 inches of oil in a deep pot until it reaches 350°F, then carefully lower the eggs, a couple at a time, into the pot. Cook until golden brown, about 5 minutes, carefully turning over at the halfway point. Use a slotted spoon to take them out and put them on paper towels to drain.

8. Slice open and enjoy.

KALUA PORK DEVILED EGGS

MAKES 24 DEVILED EGG HALVES

20 MINUTES

Deviled eggs are one of the greatest food combinations known to mankind. And what I especially love about these is that they can easily be prepped a day ahead of needing them—just don't build them until it's go-time.

12 leftover Perfectly Hard-Boiled Eggs (page 132), peeled

Roughly ⅓ cup mayonnaise

¼ cup finely diced red onion

¼ cup finely chopped green onion, white and light green parts

1 tablespoon hot sauce, such as Cholula

1 tablespoon spicy brown mustard

Kosher salt and freshly ground black pepper

About ½ cup leftover Kalua Pork (page 86)

1. Slice the eggs lengthwise down the middle (but then you knew that, right?).

2. Put the whites on your serving plate and the yolks in a bowl.

3. To the yolks, add the mayo, red onion, 3 tablespoons of the green onion, and the hot sauce, mustard, and salt and pepper to taste.

4. Mix well to combine and then fill each of the egg halves with some of the mixture (you'll have some left over, and that's cool).

5. Top each with some of the pork, and finally top with remaining green onion.

POACHED SHRIMP, AND THEN . . . .

You know those "already cooked shrimp" with shitty cocktail sauce you buy from the supermarket that come in that plastic clamshell thing? Well, they suck, and you should be embarrassed for even putting them in your cart. But I'm here for you, and not only are these ones way, way better, but look at what you can do with them after . . .

Basic Poached Shrimp
Fresh Thai Shrimp Spring Rolls
Shrimp Foo Yung
Chopped Shrimp Louie with Chipotle Dressing

BASIC POACHED SHRIMP

**MAKES 1 POUND SHRIMP
20 MINUTES**

A freshly poached shrimp will be about a thousand times better than anything you buy.

½ lemon

1½ teaspoons black peppercorns

1 bay leaf (if you have it; if not, don't worry about it)

1 teaspoon salt

1 pound unpeeled but deveined large raw shrimp; 16/20s are perfect here

Ice water

1. Fill a medium pot with water, squeeze and drop in the lemon half, and add the peppercorns, bay leaf, and salt.

2. Bring to a boil over medium heat, then remove from the heat and put in the shrimp.

3. Cover and let stand for 4 to 5 minutes, or just until the shrimp turn pink.

4. While they poach, fill a large bowl with ice water.

5. Immediately put the poached shrimp into the ice water. Let stand for 10 minutes, remove from the water, peel, and use—or don't peel and store in the fridge . . . it's totally up to you.

And while we're here poaching shrimp the right way, hopefully you're going to want to dunk them in something. And the obvious, and perhaps best thing, is simple yet delicious:

EVERYDAY GREAT COCKTAIL SAUCE

MAKES ½ CUP

½ cup chili sauce, the Western type, not the hot Asian version

1 to 2 tablespoons prepared horseradish

1 teaspoon Worcestershire sauce

½ teaspoon Cholula hot sauce

Juice of ½ lemon

1 tablespoon chopped fresh curly parsley

1. Mix everything together in a small bowl until well combined.

2. Keep refrigerated.

Butter-Poached Shrimp

Effort warning: This is a bit over the top, but I thought I'd throw it in just in case you were having King Henry VIII over for dinner. And, of course, they come out buttery but also tender, juicy, and amazing. The only real key is, you should use excellent butter. This is not the time for the budget store brand. And a European butter will be a good place to look. **MAKES 1 POUND SHRIMP**

½ pound (2 sticks)
  really good butter
1 pound 16/20 shrimp, peeled
  and deveined but tail on,
  at room temperature
Kosher salt and freshly
  ground black pepper
Chopped fresh parsley
  for garnish

1. Slowly melt the butter in a small pot over medium heat—don't boil, just keep at an almost simmer.

2. Add the shrimp so they are covered with butter; if not all will fit covered, cook them in two batches.

3. Cook until the shrimp are just done—tender, juicy, but not overdone—probably 3-ish minutes total.

4. Serve in a bowl, seasoned with salt and pepper to taste and garnished with the parsley.

5. And fine, if you have a little bread, you can always dip that, too. Just sayin' . . .

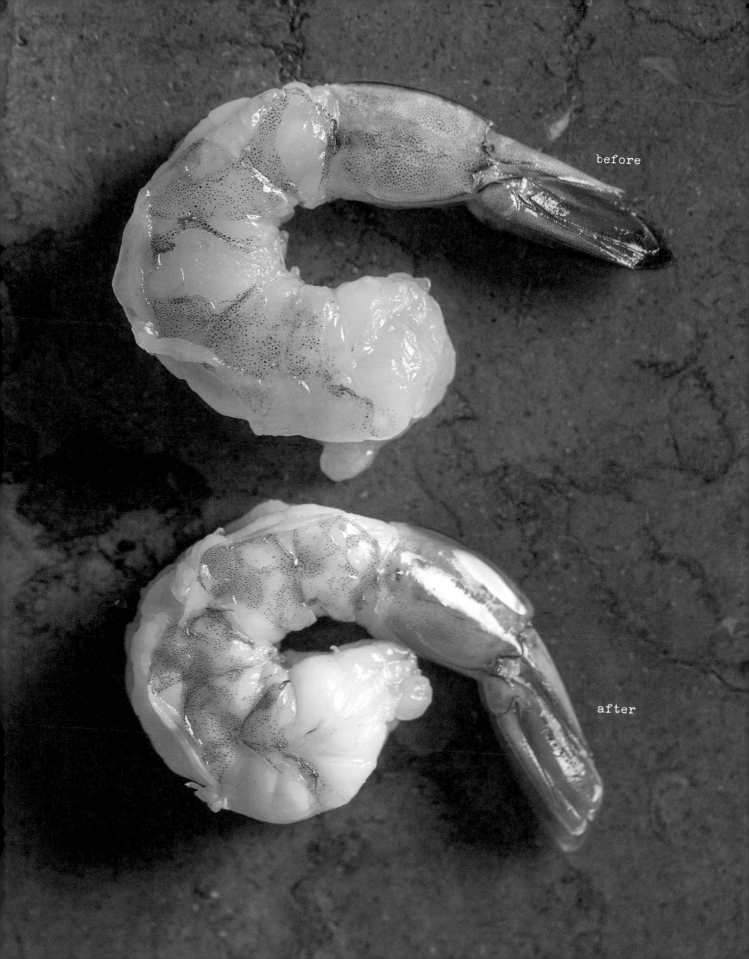

before

after

FRESH THAI SHRIMP SPRING ROLLS

MAKES 8 SPRING ROLLS
20 MINUTES

Fresh, as in not crispy or deep-fried—not that there's anything wrong with that. Those are just not these ones.

SAUCE:

3 tablespoons sweet chili sauce
2 tablespoons peanut butter
½ teaspoon soy sauce
½ teaspoon hoisin sauce
¼ teaspoon sesame oil
1 tablespoon finely
   chopped green onion

ROLLS:

2 ounces rice vermicelli
   (clear noodles)
Eight 8½-inch rice spring
   roll wrappers
1 carrot, sliced into
   thin matchsticks
½ English cucumber, sliced
   into matchsticks
Twelve 21/25 leftover
   Basic Poached Shrimp
   (page 144), cooled and
   cut in half lengthwise
⅓ cup chopped fresh Thai basil
⅓ cup chopped fresh mint leaves
⅓ cup chopped fresh cilantro
2 lettuce leaves, chopped
Peanut sauce for dipping

1. Make the sauce: Combine the sauce ingredients in a small bowl, mix well, then set aside.

2. Make the rolls: Cook the vermicelli in boiling water for about 2 minutes, then drain and rinse with cold water and set aside.

3. Put about an inch of warm water into a large dish and place one spring roll wrapper in the water. Let soak for 10 to 15 seconds. Note: If you let it soak for too long, it will become soft and impossible to use.

4. Lay the wrapper on a clean surface and place three shrimp halves, face down, horizontally across the middle. This step is important because once the wrapper is rolled up, the shrimp will be what you see and you want them to look pretty.

5. Top with some of the vermicelli, then add any of the vegetables and herbs you like on top.

6. To roll, bring the side of the spring roll closest to you tightly over top of the ingredients. Then bring in each side toward the middle, and finally roll away from you like a tight, small burrito. Repeat Steps 3–6 to make the remaining spring rolls.

7. Serve with the peanut sauce for dipping.

SHRIMP FOO YUNG

Who doesn't like a good egg foo yung? Wait—maybe I should ask, "When was the last time you even had egg foo yung?" This one with shrimp is, well, just stupid good.

½ cup chicken gravy, made or bought . . . it's all good

2 tablespoons soy sauce

6 large eggs

⅓ cup finely chopped green onions, plus more for garnish

¾ cup fresh bean sprouts

1 cup leftover Perfectly Poached Shrimp (page 144), roughly chopped

2 tablespoons oil for pan

1. Pour the gravy into a small pot, stir in the soy sauce, and keep warm over low heat.

2. Heat a large nonstick skillet over medium heat.

3. Beat the eggs really well in a medium bowl.

4. Add the green onions, bean sprouts, and shrimp to the beaten eggs and stir well.

5. Add the oil to the pan, making sure the bottom is covered, and slowly pour in the egg mixture.

6. Cook for 2 to 3 minutes, or until just set, then flip to cook the other side.

7. Once both sides are cooked, transfer to a plate and spoon some gravy over it.

8. Garnish with a little chopped green onion.

CHOPPED SHRIMP LOUIE WITH CHIPOTLE DRESSING

SERVES 2
20 MINUTES

This is a Sunday salad to me. A big, fat, delicious salad (but without mayo, so it's not as fat for you) that deserves a big, fat glass of wine—and a crisp white would go beautifully with this.

DRESSING:

¾ cup sour cream or nonfat Greek yogurt

1 chipotle chile, finely minced

Juice of ½ lime

1 teaspoon Worcestershire sauce

½ teaspoon garlic powder

Kosher salt and freshly ground black pepper

Milk for thinning (optional)

SALAD:

2 leftover Perfectly Hard-Boiled Eggs (page 132), chopped

1 romaine heart, chopped

1 medium tomato, diced

1 avocado, peeled, pitted, and diced

½ cup diced English cucumber

4 radishes, thinly sliced

8 ounces leftover Basic Poached Shrimp (page 144)

Freshly ground black pepper

Finely chopped fresh parsley for garnish

1. Make the dressing: Combine all the dressing ingredients in a small bowl and mix well. Use milk to thin it out to your preference.

2. Assemble the salad: Put all the salad ingredients except the shrimp, pepper, and parsley in a medium bowl, add about a third of the dressing (more if you prefer), and mix so everything is coated.*

3. Plate nicely, add half of the shrimp to the top of each salad, and drizzle with more dressing.

4. Add a few grinds of black pepper and garnish with parsley.

*Rather than mixing the salad in a bowl, you could always line up the ingredients on a plate and throw on the dressing Jackson Pollock-style, like I stupidly did.

SESAME CHILI SALMON, AND THEN . . .

I'm no dietitian, but as far as I can tell, salmon is about as perfect a food as it gets. It's low in calories, high in really good fat, and can be cooked so damn many ways: baked, broiled, steamed, smoked, grilled, seared, poached, stir-fried, etc. And let's not forget you can eat it just plain ol' raw. If I had to choose only one food to eat for the rest of my life, it would be salmon, no question.

Sesame Chili Salmon
Asian Salmon Salad
Sesame Chili Salmon Avotoast
Finnish Salmon Soup
Salmon BLT Sliders

SESAME CHILI SALMON

MAKES 4 SERVINGS
15 MINUTES

This is the dinner that Kelly asks me to make more than anything else. And when I do, I always make an extra piece or three for the next day to eat right outta the fridge or in any of the great recipes that follow.

Four 6-ounce salmon fillets
   (Kelly prefers skin off,
   but either way will do)
Kosher salt and freshly
   ground black pepper
6 tablespoons sesame chili oil*
¼ cup finely chopped
   green onion

1. Put the salmon on a plate and season well with salt and pepper on both sides and drizzle with the sesame chili oil on both sides—let sit a couple of minutes.

2. Heat a medium nonstick skillet really well over medium-high heat (until almost smoking), turn on your fan, and add the salmon, face down.**

3. Let cook without moving it until you see it has cooked approximately one-third of the way up the side.

4. Carefully flip it over, and repeat—it will take less time on this side, but depending on how thick your salmon is, it could take 5 to 6 minutes total to cook both sides.

5. I like to serve it on fresh steamed rice with the green onions as garnish.

*You can buy sesame chili oil at almost any Asian market. And if you can't find it, buy sesame oil and chili oil separately and just combine the two.

**When searing anything, the presentation side (the side that will be face up on the plate) always goes face down first because that's when the pan is at its cleanest and hottest and will give the prettiest sear. Am I here for you or what?

ASIAN SALMON SALAD

Our dinner routine is almost the same every night—the same routine, not the same food. It goes like this: I call Kelly at work or ask if she's at home, "What do you feel like for dinner?" And most of the time the answer is: "Salad with . . . ," and most of those times it's with this crispy salmon cuz it's so damn good. Salad for dinner plain—not for me. Salad for dinner with this—hell yes. And because I have no idea, this is more about the dressing and what I put in the salad.

DRESSING:
⅔ cup neutral oil
3 tablespoons rice vinegar
2 tablespoons soy sauce
½ teaspoon sesame oil
1 teaspoon sriracha
Pinch of kosher salt

SALAD:
Leaves—baby arugula or
   spinach is perfect here
Cucumbers—thinly sliced
Radishes—thinly sliced
Edamame
English peas, raw—I'm always
   amazed at how many people
   have never had them raw
   right out of the shell
Snow peas—diagonally sliced
Raw cauliflower—finely chopped
Shiitake mushrooms—thinly
   sliced and cooked in a little
   oil until soft and luxurious
Leftover Sesame Chili
   Salmon (page 156)
Sesame chili oil for
   drizzling (optional)
Seeds—toasted sesame
   or pine nuts
Diced green onion

1. Make the dressing: Put all the dressing ingredients in a bowl or dressing shaker and mix well to combine. Refrigerate until needed.

2. Assemble the salad: Put all the salad ingredients except the salmon, chili oil, seeds, and green onion in a bowl (and a cool-looking wooden bowl to serve out of wouldn't suck here).

3. Add a small amount of dressing and mix—you can always add more.

4. Plate, top with the salmon, maybe add a small drizzle of sesame chili oil, and garnish with a few sesame seeds and diced green onion.

SESAME CHILI SALMON AVOTOAST

This is one of my favorite food starts to the day.

4 slices of a really great,
   seedy bread

2 small avocados,
   peeled and pitted

4 to 6 ounces leftover Sesame
   Chili Salmon (page 156)

Togarashi Japanese
   spice blend*

Kosher salt

Roughly chopped fresh
   cilantro (or, if you're going
   to serve this for something
   fancier than just eating
   it in the kitchen in your
   jammies, you might want to
   consider micro cilantro—
   cuz that stuff's the shit
   and you'll look like a pro)

1. Toast the bread.

2. Put each avocado half on each piece of toast and lightly mash with the back of a fork—do not turn into a gross paste.

3. Carefully break apart the salmon (keeping it mostly recognizable, if possible) and add to avocado.

4. Season with togarashi and kosher salt and top with cilantro.

*I know I'll get shit for going Martha Stewart on you and suggesting a random spice your supermarket probably won't have, but two things: The first is I'm trying to up your food game, and having togarashi around will made a lot of things a lot more interesting. And second, there's this thing called the Internet—and it can probably send this to you before you finish reading the recipe. So there.

FINNISH SALMON SOUP

I spent about a week in Finland a few years ago, and this soup was everywhere—and for good reason cuz it's so good. And the fact that we're starting with a spicy version of the salmon will just make it better.

2 small leeks, cleaned and thinly sliced—just the white and light green parts

2 tablespoons butter

5 cups fish stock (chicken or vegetable stock will work, but try to find fish stock if you can)

1 pound fingerling potatoes, sliced crosswise into ¼-inch slices

3 small carrots, sliced crosswise into ¼-inch slices

1 cup heavy cream

½ to ¾ pound leftover Sesame Chili Salmon (page 156)

¾ cup finely chopped fresh dill

Kosher salt and freshly ground black pepper

5-Minute Beer Bread (page 242) for serving (optional)

1. Cook the leeks in butter over medium heat in a medium saucepan until just softened, about 5 minutes.

2. Add the stock, potatoes, and carrots and bring to a boil, then lower the heat to a simmer.

3. Let cook for 10 to 12 minutes, until the vegetables have softened.

4. Add the cream and cook for about 5 minutes, or until slightly thickened. Then, add the salmon and dill and let warm through.

5. Season to taste with salt and pepper.

6. Cover with a lid and let sit for 5 or so minutes or more. Serve ideally with leftover 5-Minute Beer Bread.

SALMON BLT SLIDERS

A platter of these for a game, a game night, or just an afternoon hang will make everyone happy.

¼ cup mayonnaise

Juice of ½ lemon

1 small garlic clove, minced

⅛ teaspoon smoked paprika

4 Hawaiian rolls

4 slices Roma tomato

½ cup shredded iceberg lettuce

4 slices bacon, cooked
   until crisp

6 ounces leftover Sesame
   Chili Salmon (page 156),
   at room temperature

1. Put the mayo, lemon juice, garlic, and paprika in a small bowl. Stir well.

2. Lightly toast the buns, add some of the mayo mixture to the bottom halves, plus lettuce, tomato, bacon, salmon, and the top bun.

3. Kick back and enjoy.

GRILLED OR OVEN-ROASTED VEGETABLES, AND THEN . . .

If parents only knew how
incredibly amazing roasted
or grilled veggies were when
compared to boiled or microwaved
ones . . . the expression "eat
your vegetables" would never have
shown up in the English language.
Ever.

Basic but Delicious Grilled Vegetables
Grilled Veggie Burger
Pasta with Veggies
Grilled Veggie Pizza
Roasted Veggie Crostini

BASIC BUT DELICIOUS GRILLED VEGETABLES

MBOWYG

30 MINUTES

Grilled veggies make almost everything better and are pretty much a snap to make. The recipe that follows will make enough for a week. (Kidding!)

5 tablespoons butter

⅓ cup oil

¼ cup Dijon mustard

6 teaspoons finely chopped mixed fresh herbs,* such as thyme, rosemary, and parsley

2 garlic cloves, finely minced

Kosher salt and freshly ground black pepper

4 green zucchini or yellow summer squash, sliced lengthwise into ½-inch planks

2 red bell peppers, seeded and sides sliced off

2 yellow bell peppers, seeded and sides sliced off

2 red onions, peeled and cut into ½-inch-thick rounds

2 large carrots, peeled, then cut into ⅓- to 2-inch planks

2 portobello mushrooms

2 eggplants, cut into ½-inch-thick rounds

1 pound asparagus, thick ends removed

Grill spray

1. Preheat a grill or grill pan to medium-high.**

2. Combine the butter, oil, mustard, herbs, garlic, and salt and black pepper to taste in a small pot. Heat, stirring, over medium heat until the butter has melted and the mixture is well blended. Remove from the heat.

3. Brush the vegetables lightly with the butter mixture and season with salt and black pepper to taste. Reserve the remaining butter mixture.

4. Heat a grill to medium-high, spray with grill spray, and add the vegetables.

5. Then just cook, basting with extra butter as you go until all are still a little crisp-tender but lightly charred all over.

6. Since different vegetables cook at different times, just remove as each is done.

**No grill or grill pan, no sweat. Just heat your oven to 425°F, put the veggies on a baking sheet, brush lightly with the butter mixture, season with salt and black pepper, and cook for about 10 minutes, or until still crisp-tender.

*If you only have dried, that's cool, too; just use about half the measurement of each.

GRILLED VEGGIE BURGER

Veggie burgers are often made of nuts, grains, and similar non-vegetable-looking things. And not that there's anything wrong with that, but wtf? Mine is made with actual—wait for it—"real"' vegetables . . . because how do you grill a handful of bulgur wheat?

1 tablespoon basil pesto

1 tablespoon soft goat cheese

Any combination of leftover Basic but Delicious Grilled Vegetables (page 168)— your goal is to have about an inch or so worth of the veggies on a bun

Oil for brushing

1 sourdough, brioche, or some kind of good bun*

1. Combine the pesto and goat cheese in a small bowl, mix well, and set aside.

2. Reheat the veggies: give them a light brushing of oil and then 5 minutes or so in a 350°F oven or a few minutes in a nonstick skillet over medium heat.

3. Split the bun and toast it lightly.

4. Spread the pesto mixture on the bottom bun, then add the veggies and the top half.

```
*I feel the need to discuss bun and
bread quality here cuz it's often
overlooked. Wait, make that often
completely ignored. It kills me when
someone takes the time to make something
great but then serves it in or with a
lousy bread product—so don't do that.
Don't just grab some lame-ass thing cuz
it's on sale. A little thought here will
make all the difference.
```

PASTA WITH VEGGIES

SERVES 4
20 MINUTES

I love this pasta for a couple of reasons: the first is just how good it is, and the second is that it's not a heavy, creamy, saucy, fatty version. It's fresh from all the veggies mixed with just garlic oil. Oh and feel free to swap up the veggies like the recipe says. You don't have to be all fancy, like I did for the pic.

VEGETABLES:

2 tablespoons oil

3 cups roughly chopped leftover Basic but Delicious Grilled Vegetables (page 168)

PASTA:

1 pound pasta—your choice, but I like spaghetti for this one

¼ cup olive oil

4 garlic cloves, thinly sliced

Chopped fresh parsley

Shredded Parmesan

2 teaspoons red pepper flakes

Freshly ground black pepper

1. Make the vegetables: Heat a medium skillet over medium-high heat, add the oil and, when hot, add the vegetables to reheat and even make a little crispy, then turn down and keep warm.

2. Meanwhile, make the pasta: cook according to the package directions.

3. Heat the olive oil in a separate skillet over medium-low heat (but not too hot).

4. Add the sliced garlic to the oil and lightly brown for maybe 2 minutes. (Do not overbrown or it will become bitter.)

5. Drain the cooked pasta, transfer to a bowl, pour in the olive oil and garlic, and stir well to mix.

6. Sprinkle with some chopped parsley and mix through, then add the vegetables and stir well.

7. To serve, put some pasta onto a plate and sprinkle with a bit more of the parsley and some Parmesan. Season with red pepper flakes and black pepper to taste.

8. That's it—simple.

GRILLED VEGGIE PIZZA

This pizza is one of the reasons I decided to write this book in the first place. I had some grilled veggies in the fridge one night, I was thinking about what to make for dinner, and I turned them into a pizza. And somewhere around bite six or seven, the light went off in my head . . .

1 ball pizza dough

1½ cups roughly chopped leftover Basic but Delicious Grilled Vegetables (page 168)

3 ounces crumbled goat or feta cheese

½ to 1 teaspoon red pepper flakes

Kosher salt and freshly ground black pepper

Extra-virgin olive oil

1. Preheat the oven to 450°F.

2. Spread the pizza dough into approximately a 12-inch circle* on a large baking sheet and bake for 5 minutes.

3. Remove from the oven and top with the veggies, crumbled cheese, red pepper flakes, and salt and black pepper to taste.

4. Put back in the oven and bake for another 10 to 12 minutes, until the crust is golden and the toppings are hot.

5. Remove from the oven and drizzle lightly with olive oil.

6. Slice, of course, and serve.

*Or whatever shape you end up with cuz, frankly, a perfectly round pizza is a lot harder to achieve than it looks. So, if you end up with anything other than a circle (which you likely will), just call it "rustic" and they'll think you're Julia Child.

ROASTED VEGGIE CROSTINI

Here's the deal—crispy warm baguette, smooth garlicky ricotta, and Leftover Basic but Delicious Grilled Vegetables make for one amazing appetizer.

¾ cup ricotta

1 large garlic clove

½ sourdough baguette, sliced into ½-inch rounds

Olive oil

About 1 cup roughly chopped leftover Basic but Delicious Grilled Vegetables (page 168)

Parmesan, grated or shredded, for garnish

1. Preheat the broiler to high .

2. Put the ricotta and garlic in a small bowl and mix until well combined, then set aside.

3. Place the baguette rounds on a baking sheet, brush lightly with olive oil, and put about 6 inches under the broiler until just getting golden and crispy (btw, you can easily do this part ahead of time; just be sure not to get them too crispy cuz they'll get crispier as they sit).

4. Remove from the broiler, spread each with some of the ricotta mixture, top with veggies, and garnish with Parmesan.

5. Put back under the broiler for about 2 minutes, then remove and serve.

ROASTED RED PEPPER SAUCE, AND THEN . . . .

Just gonna say it—this is one of
the most useful recipes in this
book. A frozen container of this
in your freezer will soon become
your best friend.

Roasted Red Pepper Sauce

Roasted Red Pepper Soup

The Best Thing That Ever
Happened to a Piece of Fish

10-Minute Red Pepper Gazpacho

Amazing Bacon, Onion & Fried Egg Toast

ROASTED RED PEPPER SAUCE

MAKES ABOUT 2 CUPS SAUCE
15 MINUTES

However much you think you need, you should make more cuz you can use the hell outta this.

½ yellow onion, diced

1 tablespoon oil

1 large garlic clove

One 15-ounce jar roasted red peppers, drained

¼ teaspoon cayenne pepper

½ teaspoon salt

5 grinds black pepper

2 tablespoons chicken stock or water

1. Cook the onion in the oil in a medium pot over medium heat until softened, about 5 minutes.

2. Add the garlic and cook until fragrant, about a minute more, then add the drained peppers. Stir well.

3. Your goal now is to blend it into a smooth sauce. For this, you can use either a processor, a regular blender, or even an immersion blender. Whatever you choose, add the cayenne, salt, black pepper, and the stock, and process or blend until smooth.

4. Use or freeze.

5. No—you should use.

ROASTED RED PEPPER SOUP

MBOWYG

5 MINUTES

The difference between this and the Roasted Red Pepper Sauce is the thickness and the toppings. Kelly loves this so much that I always keep a couple deli containers of it in the freezer. Remember how in the beginning I said some of these will be less recipe, more suggestion? Well, this is more suggestion because it's so easy.

Leftover Roasted Red Pepper Sauce (page 180)—about 1½ cups per person
Chicken stock, for thinning

1. Put the sauce in a pot over medium heat and let it warm a bit—it will thin out as it heats up.

2. After about 5 minutes, if it's still too thick, add some stock, a little at a time, until it gets to where you like it.

At this point you have roasted red pepper soup, and it'll be delicious. But to really make you happy, try adding any or all of these:

- A spoonful of sour cream
- Chopped green onions
- Chopped fresh cilantro
- Garlic Croutons (page 250)
- Pumpkin seeds or pine nuts
- Crispy onions
- Sautéed onions

THE BEST THING THAT EVER HAPPENED TO A PIECE OF FISH

With pretty much only two main ingredients (the fish and the roasted red pepper sauce), this is definitely "less of a recipe and more of a teaching moment." And here's the short version: cook a piece of fish, put some of the Roasted Red Pepper Sauce on it, and fall in love.

Pretty much any fish will work: salmon, cod, sea bass, halibut, even scallops

Oil

Kosher salt and freshly ground black pepper

Leftover Roasted Red Pepper Sauce (page 180)

Extra-virgin olive oil for finishing

Fresh lemon juice

Fresh cilantro, parsley, or basil for garnish

1. Pat the fish dry with paper towels, oil lightly, season with salt and black pepper, and cook: grill, pan sear, broil, poach, smoke—it's up to you (don't microwave, though; that would really suck)—but this brings me to a point.*

2. When the fish is done, plate it and serve with some of the red pepper sauce, a drizzle of olive oil, and a squeeze of lemon. Garnish with something green.

*Fish at home—amazing. Fish rewarmed at work the next day in the office microwave should be outlawed. Really.

10-MINUTE RED PEPPER GAZPACHO

SERVES 4 TO 6
10 MINUTES

This is another one of our faves, and it goes great with shrimp—which maybe you've already made from the poached shrimp chapter.

2 garlic cloves, peeled

2 yellow bell peppers, seeded and cut into big chunks

1 medium yellow onion, cut into big chunks

1 long English cucumber, cut lengthwise and then into 1-inch chunks (you can use regular cucumbers, but you need to peel and seed them . . . it's just not worth it)

Leaves from 1 large bunch cilantro or parsley

2 tablespoons hot sauce (I like Cholula)

2 cups leftover Roasted Red Pepper Sauce (page 180), cold or room temperature—just not warm

Kosher salt and freshly ground black pepper

Extra-virgin olive oil for serving

1. The key is to blend everything, so if it will all fit in a processor or blender the first time, go ahead and blend, according to the next steps, until still a bit chunky. If not, do it in two shifts; eventually everything will fit for the final blend with the red pepper sauce.

2. Put the garlic in the processor and blitz for a couple of seconds.

3. Add the bell peppers and onion and blitz for about 5 seconds.

4. Add the cucumber and your preferred herb, and blitz again for about 5 seconds.

5. Now add the hot sauce and red pepper sauce, and blend to bring everything together, but keep it a little chunky.

6. Transfer to a bowl, stir in salt and black pepper to taste, and drizzle with a little olive oil.

AMAZING BACON, ONION & FRIED EGG TOAST

THIS SERVES 1, SO DOUBLE OR TRIPLE AS NECESSARY

10 MINUTES

This might be one of the greatest egg combos ever. And I don't really want to tell you how to cook the egg for this, but I will: a runny yolk is everything here, so make it over easy or sunny-side up.

2 strips bacon, cut in half

¼ yellow onion, sliced thinnish

1 large egg

1 slice bread—btw, the 5-Minute Beer Bread (page 242) would be ideal here

¼ cup leftover Roasted Red Pepper Sauce (page 180), warmed up

Freshly ground black pepper (optional)

1. Cook the bacon in a large nonstick skillet until three-quarters of the way done.

2. Push the bacon to one side, add the onion to the pan, and cook it in the bacon grease—two slices won't make too much grease, so don't freak out.

3. When the onion has softened, slide the bacon and onion over to one side, and crack the egg into the remaining grease and cook . . . you know how.

4. Toast the bread.

5. When the egg is done, put the toast on a plate and top with the bacon, onion, and egg.

6. Immediately add the red pepper sauce to the pan to heat it up, then drizzle over the egg.

7. Maybe a few grinds of pepper, and whammo—effing deliciousness!

FRIES & 3 SAUCES, AND THEN . . .

Oh sure, you can just buy
fries from almost anywhere, and
they'll probably be delicious.
But knowing how to make your own
is not just a fun party trick—
it's essential for so many
dishes. And no matter how you get
them, having leftovers will be
important for making these:

Ridiculously Good Fries
Cali Breakfast Burrito
Breakfast (French Fry) Hash Browns
Weekend Fry-Tatta

RIDICULOUSLY GOOD FRIES

Is this a bit more work than buying fries? Of course. But is it worth it? Double of course. Because when you take still-sizzling fries out of the oil, season them right away with sea salt, and have a bite, you're going to burn yourself for sure. So wait a minute but then . . . heaven. Pure fry heaven.

MAKES AS MANY AS YOU WANT (OR NEED), BUT YOU'LL GET ABOUT 2 SERVINGS PER POUND OF POTATOES

30 MINUTES

Russet potatoes
Vegetable or peanut oil for frying
Sea salt
Dipping sauces: ketchup, mayo,* Curry Ketchup, Pepper Ketchup, Fry Sauce

*The Dutch and Canadians eat fries with mayo and it's amazing.

1. Peel one potato, slice into planks lengthwise and then into sticks, and immediately put them in a bowl of cold water to keep them from turning brown. Repeat with the remaining potatoes. Let them soak for about an hour.

2. When ready, drain the potatoes on paper towels really, really, really well because wet fries and hot oil are nothing you want to be involved with.

3. Fill a deep fryer or large, heavy pot with about 3 inches of oil and heat. Note: Do not crowd the fryer with too many fries—a crowded pot is no *bueno*. So cook the fries in batches at 350°F for 5 minutes. Remove them and drain again on fresh paper towels.

4. Once all the potatoes have been cooked, you'll cook them a second time. Increase the oil temperature to 375°F, and when it's there, fry again in batches until they're golden and crisp.

5. Remove, drain again on paper towels, put in a bowl, immediately sprinkle with salt, and go for it.

CURRY KETCHUP

½ cup ketchup
1½ teaspoons curry powder
1 teaspoon paprika

1. Mix together.
2. Use.

(continues)

PEPPER KETCHUP

Ketchup
Freshly ground black pepper

1. Put the ketchup in a small ramekin and cover with so much pepper that you don't see any red.

2. Dip in a fry and say, "Thank you, Sam."

FRY SAUCE*

½ cup mayonnaise
¼ cup ketchup
1 tablespoon Cholula hot sauce (or whatever kind you like)
1 regular-size dill pickle, diced very small
2 tablespoons dill pickle juice
Kosher salt and freshly ground black pepper

1. Put all the ingredients in a bowl and mix well to combine.

2. Store in the fridge for a couple of weeks.

*Also amazing on burgers!

The Proper Way to Reheat Leftover Fries—Basic, Yes, but Very Important

Any amount of fries

1. Turn on your broiler.

2. Meanwhile, put the fries on a microwave-safe plate—mostly spread out, not in a giant mound.

3. Microwave on HIGH for 15 to 20 seconds until warm.

4. Immediately transfer the fries to a baking sheet and put under the broiler 5 or 6 inches from the heat.

5. Watch them very carefully, shaking the pan every minute or so for even heating.

6. When they're hot, crispy, and beautiful—they're done.

CALI BREAKFAST BURRITOS

MAKES 4 BURRITOS
15 MINUTES

I'm from San Diego, where the California burrito is more religion than food. And the thing that makes it a Cali burrito is the fries. Is this more work for something that highlights fries? Maybe. But you just got a fricking tremendous carne asada recipe at the same time.

⅓ cup sour cream

1½ teaspoons finely minced chipotle chile

1 pound raw boneless short ribs, very thinly sliced

1 teaspoon dried oregano

1 teaspoon garlic powder

1 teaspoon ground cumin

1 teaspoon kosher salt

2 tablespoons soy sauce

2 tablespoons finely chopped fresh cilantro

1 tablespoon oil

4 large eggs, beaten

4 burrito-size tortillas

1 cup shredded Monterey Jack

4 handfuls leftover Ridiculously Good Fries (page 192)

⅓ cup pico de gallo (fresh salsa)

½ cup guacamole

1. Combine the sour cream and chipotle in a small bowl, mix well, and set aside.

2. Put the short ribs in a separate bowl along with the oregano, garlic powder, cumin, salt, soy sauce, cilantro, and oil. Mix well to combine, and if you have a couple of hours, cover and put in the fridge. If you don't . . . forge ahead Sparky, and you'll be fine.

3. Heat a flat griddle or skillet over high heat, add the sliced rib meat (let any excess marinade drip off before putting the ribs in the pan), and cook until just done. This cooks fast, probably 2 minutes. Remove from the heat and keep warm.

4. Cook the eggs in a nonstick pan over medium heat until just done.

5. Warm the tortillas and build your burritos: Place each tortilla flat in front of you and add some of the short rib, then top with one-quarter of the eggs, cheese, fries, pico, guac, and finally top with some of the sour cream sauce.

6. Once you have all the fillings in place, bring the bottom half of each tortilla closest to you over the top to cover the insides. Pull the top toward you to form a tight roll. Now fold the two sides in towards the middle, and then tightly roll the whole thing away from you.

BREAKFAST (FRENCH FRY) HASH BROWNS

SERVES 1, PROBABLY
15 MINUTES

It occurred to me one Sunday morning, when I was thinking about making brunch, that I didn't have any potatoes for hash browns, but I did have some leftover fries from the night before—and that's all I needed . . .

2 tablespoons oil

½ red bell pepper, seeded and diced small

½ green bell pepper, seeded and diced small

⅓ cup small-diced red onion

¼ cup finely chopped green onion

1 garlic clove, minced

2 cups chopped leftover Ridiculously Good Fries (page 192)

½ teaspoon kosher salt

¼ teaspoon freshly ground black pepper

¼ teaspoon red pepper flakes

1. Heat the oil in a large cast-iron or nonstick skillet over medium heat and add the bell peppers and onions. Cook until softened.

2. Add the garlic and cook until fragrant, about 30 seconds.

3. Add the chopped-up fries, season with the salt, black pepper, and pepper flakes, mix well, then press down flat into a large pancake kind of thing.

4. Lower the heat to medium-low and cook the hash browns until crispy and browned on both sides—maybe 10 minutes per side.

5. Serve—and putting a couple of cooked eggs on top wouldn't suck.

WEEKEND FRY-TATTA

This is simply using something you already have and turning it into something even more delicious.

8 large eggs

½ teaspoon kosher salt

¼ teaspoon freshly
    ground black pepper

½ cup shredded Monterey Jack

8 ounces bacon, diced

8 ounces cremini mushrooms,
    stemmed and thinly sliced

1 garlic clove, minced

1½ cups leftover Ridiculously
    Good Fries (page 192)

Sour cream for serving

Hot sauce for serving

1. Preheat the oven to 350°F.

2. Beat the eggs in a bowl, add the salt and pepper, and stir in the cheese.

3. Cook the bacon in a 10-inch cast-iron or ovenproof nonstick pan over medium heat.

4. When it's about halfway done, remove half of the grease, then add the mushrooms and cook until they soften, about 3 minutes.

5. Add the garlic and cook, stirring, until it becomes very fragrant, about a minute, then add the fries and stir so they get coated with everything.

6. Pour in the egg mixture and stir slightly to make sure everything is evenly distributed. Then leave undisturbed so the bottom starts to set, about 3 minutes.

7. Transfer the pan to the oven and let bake until the eggs are fully set, 13 to 15 minutes.

8. I like to serve warm or at room temperature with a spoonful of sour cream and a splash or two of hot sauce.

MASHED POTATOES, AND THEN . . .

There are things in life you
must know how to make—and mashed
potatoes are definitely one of
them. And once you know how,
make extra.

Mashed Potatoes
Kalua Pork Shepherd's Pie
Mashed Potato Tacos
Potato Bacon Rolls
Grilled Leftover Steak & Mashed Potato Pizza
Quick Cheater Pierogi

MASHED POTATOES

I can hear someone yelling now, "Hey, this idiot is telling us how to make mashed potatoes . . . what a dope!" But it's not stupid because this simple little recipe will not just make a Thanksgiving meal perfect—it will improve so many other dishes as well. Really, it's about the small things in life.

3 pounds Yukon Gold potatoes
¾ cup heavy cream
4 tablespoons (½ stick) butter
1 garlic clove, really
   finely minced
Kosher salt and freshly
   ground black pepper

1. Fill a large pot about halfway with water and put over medium heat.

2. Peel potatoes, one at a time, and slice into equal-size pieces— big or small doesn't matter, but they need to be the same size so they'll evenly cook in the pot at the same time. Put them into the pot as you slice so they don't turn brown.

3. Simmer until soft enough to put a fork into, about 15 minutes.

4. While they cook, combine the cream, butter, and garlic in a small pot and heat over medium-low heat until the butter has melted. Then turn off the heat.

5. When the potatoes are done, drain really well and then mash in the pot—I like to use a potato ricer because it makes the smoothest potatoes.

6. Once mashed, stir the cream and butter in really well and season with salt and pepper.

7. Boom!

KALUA PORK SHEPHERD'S PIE

SERVES 4 TO 6
45 MINUTES

Technically shepherd's pie is made with lamb—and we're changing that.

1 tablespoon oil
½ yellow onion, diced
1 large garlic clove
1 tablespoon tomato paste
2 tablespoons all-purpose flour
½ cup beef stock
1 teaspoon Worcestershire sauce
About 2 cups shredded leftover Kalua Pork (page 86)
1 cup cut frozen vegetables (they make interesting combos these days; look for one)
2 tablespoons chopped fresh parsley
1 teaspoon kosher salt
1 teaspoon freshly ground black pepper
2 cups leftover Mashed Potatoes (page 204)
Thanksgiving-style crispy onions (optional)

1. Preheat the oven to 400°F.

2. Heat the oil in a large, ovenproof skillet (cast iron is ideal) and cook the onion until translucent, about 3 minutes. Add the garlic and cook until fragrant, about 45 seconds or so.

3. Mix in the tomato paste, then sprinkle with the flour and mix well about a minute. Stir in the stock and Worcestershire and mix well; add a little more stock if it's too thick, but you don't want it runny.

4. Add the pork, vegetables, and parsley. Mix well until heated through, then season to taste with salt and pepper.

5. Evenly spread the leftover mashed potatoes over the mixture—you might want to even make a cool design on top with the back of a fork or something.

6. Bake for 25 to 30 minutes, until the potatoes are just beginning to brown.

7. Remove, scatter with crispy onions (if using), and let cool a bit before serving.

MASHED POTATO TACOS

MAKES 4 TACOS

5 MINUTES

From the day we opened Not Not Tacos, these were a hit. Don't laugh at the idea here's exactly how we make them in the restaurant.

Four 6-inch flour tortillas

¼ cup sour cream

1 cup leftover Mashed Potatoes (page 204), heated

Hot sauce—I like Cholula here

1½ tablespoons finely diced green onion

½ cup potato chips—the extra-crunchy kettle kind

1. Warm the tortillas in a nonstick skillet until just beginning to get some color.

2. Build the tacos in this order: tortilla, sour cream on the tortilla, mashed potatoes, drizzle of Cholula, green onion, and finally some of the chips crunched and dropped on top.

3. Eat and repeat.

POTATO BACON ROLLS

Hell yes, who couldn't love these? Sure, they take a little while, but boy oh boy. And when was the last time you made any kind of bread roll?

1 cup leftover Mashed Potatoes (page 204)

½ cup + 2 tablespoons hot milk

One ¼-ounce packet active dry yeast

¼ cup warm water (not hot, around 110°F)

6 tablespoons sugar

½ cup crumbled cooked bacon

2 large eggs

8 tablespoons (1 stick) butter, melted

2 teaspoons garlic powder

1¼ teaspoons salt

4½ cups all-purpose flour

Oil for bowl and baking dish, or cooking spray

1. Put the mashed potatoes and milk in the bowl of a mixer fitted with a dough hook. Mix until blended, then let cool until only warm.

2. Add the yeast, warm water, and 2 tablespoons of the sugar. Mix well again and cover, then let it sit for 10 minutes.

3. Add the bacon, eggs, remaining 4 tablespoons of sugar, melted butter, garlic powder, and salt and mix well again.

4. Start adding the flour, ½ cup at a time, until all of it has been mixed in, or until the dough comes away from the sides of the bowl.

5. Lightly oil a large bowl, transfer the dough to the oiled bowl, cover with a clean kitchen towel, and put in a warm place for about an hour, or until doubled in size.

6. Remove the cover and, using your hand, give the dough a couple of punches to deflate it.

7. Divide the dough into about 16 equal pieces, roll each into a ball, and space evenly apart in a 9-by-13-inch baking dish that's been lightly oiled or sprayed with cooking spray.

8. Cover and let rise until doubled, 30 minutes to an hour. Preheat the oven to 350°F.

9. Bake for 25 minutes, or until the rolls are golden on top and you can't handle the glorious aroma anymore.

GRILLED LEFTOVER STEAK & MASHED POTATO PIZZA

MAKES 1 PIZZA
45 MINUTES

Grilling makes pizza great—the steak and mashed potatoes make it greater.

1 ball pizza dough

1 tablespoon minced garlic

¼ teaspoon kosher salt

½ cup mayonnaise

3 tablespoons olive oil

1½ teaspoons fresh lemon juice

1 tablespoon finely chopped fresh parsley

Nonstick spray for grill

1 cup leftover Mashed Potatoes (page 204)

8 ounces leftover Reverse Sear (page 74), thinly sliced

¾ cup shredded smoked Gouda

1. Remove the dough from the fridge about 30 minutes before using.

2. Make the aioli: Combine the garlic, salt, mayo, 1 tablespoon of the oil, lemon juice, and parsley in a small bowl. Mix well, then cover and refrigerate.

3. Heat a grill to medium.

4. Use 1 tablespoon of the oil to oil a baking sheet. Spread the dough into about a 12-inch circle on the oiled pan.

5. Spray a grill with nonstick spray, carefully lift dough and put it oiled side down, on the grill. Lower the heat to low.

6. Once the bottom of the dough has good grill marks, 5 to 7 minutes, brush the top with the remaining tablespoon of oil and flip over.

7. Warm the mashed potatoes in a small pot or microwave to soften.

8. Leaving the crust on the grill, spread the mashed potatoes on top of the crust, then add a layer of the aioli (about 3 tablespoons), then the steak, and finally top with the Gouda.

9. Close the grill lid and let cook until the cheese melts, 3 or 4 more minutes.

10. Remove from the grill, slice, and eat—but that was obvious, right?

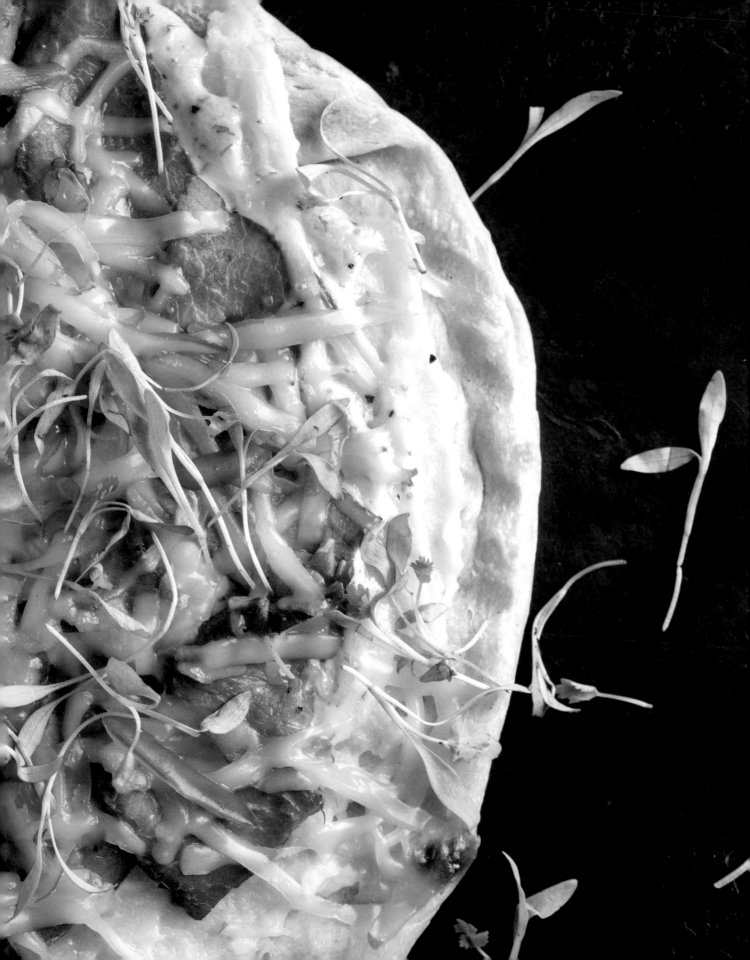

QUICK CHEATER PIEROGI

MAKES ABOUT 18 PIEROGI

30 MINUTES

Fine, I'm a cheater—I admit it. But these are much easier than making full-blown pierogi yourself, and still so good.

4 tablespoons (½ stick) butter

½ large yellow onion, thinly sliced

1 cup leftover Mashed Potatoes (page 204)

¼ cup soft goat cheese

½ teaspoon kosher salt

½ teaspoon freshly ground black pepper

18 round wonton wrappers

¾ cup sour cream for serving

Fried onions for serving

1. Melt 2 tablespoons of the butter in a nonstick pan over medium heat and add the onion. Cook until softened and just starting to brown, then remove from the heat and set aside until ready to serve.

2. Bring a large pot of water to a boil.

3. Combine mashed potatoes, cheese, salt, and pepper in a bowl and mix well.

4. Put about a tablespoon of the potato mixture in the middle of each wonton wrapper.

5. Dip your finger in water and lightly wet the wrapper edge all the way around. Fold over (making a half-moon) and seal the edges well, squeezing out as much air as possible.

6. Boil in the water about 2 minutes, or until they float.

7. Remove from the pot and drain.

8. Heat a large skillet over medium heat, melt the remaining 2 tablespoons of butter, then add the pierogi and cook until browned and getting crispy on both sides.

9. Serve with the sour cream and fried onion.

EASY PERFECT STEAMED RICE, AND THEN . . .

My wife, Kelly, called this a "silly" chapter. "Steamed rice, you're kidding, right??" she asked. Well, according to Wikipedia, "Rice is the staple food of more than half of the world's population" and, by leaving this chapter out, I would risk pissing off about 4 billion people. Who's silly now, Kelly?

Perfectly Steamed Rice

Gochujang Fried Rice

Salmon Breakfast Bowl

Fried Rice Pancakes

Chicken Soup with Rice, Lemon & Dill

PERFECTLY STEAMED RICE

MAKES 3 CUPS RICE
20 MINUTES

I've had a lot of effed-up rice, and I don't like it. And considering you're only about 20 minutes away from perfect rice, there's no excuse. And for planning purposes, 1 cup of uncooked rice will make 3 cups cooked.

1 cup uncooked basmati rice
2 cups cold water
Pinch of kosher salt

1. Put the rice in a pot that has a lid, cover with water, run your fingers through it, and then drain the rice well.

2. Cover the rice with the cold water, add a pinch of salt, bring to boil, then lower the heat to a low simmer and cover.

3. After 10 minutes, turn off the heat and let stand for 5 more minutes, then fluff and use.

GOCHUJANG FRIED RICE

The key to fried rice is using cold rice—preferably day old—so plan accordingly Sparky. And this version has one of my favorite ingredients anywhere: gochujang, pronounced "go-chew-jong," which is a Korean red pepper paste. It's a little spicy, but it's a lot good.

8 ounces bacon, diced

½ small yellow onion, diced

1 red bell pepper, seeded and diced

⅓ cup raw or frozen peas

2 cups shredded cabbage

1 large egg

½ teaspoon sesame oil

1 tablespoon soy sauce

2 garlic cloves, finely minced

1 tablespoon finely minced fresh ginger

3 cups cold leftover Perfectly Steamed Rice (page 218)

2 to 3 tablespoons gochujang

2 green onions, chopped

1. Heat a wok over medium heat and cook the bacon until about halfway to being crispy. Take out most of fat but leave a couple of tablespoons in the wok. Add the onion, bell pepper, peas, and cabbage and cook until everything softens, about 5 minutes.

2. Meanwhile, beat the egg in a small bowl and stir in the sesame oil and soy sauce; set aside.

3. Add the garlic and ginger to the wok and cook for about 1 minute, or until fragrant.

4. Crumble the rice into the wok, breaking it up, and cook until it's very hot throughout.

5. Pour in the beaten egg and mix until the egg is cooked through–about a minute.

6. Add the gochujang and stir really well to combine everything.

7. Serve, garnished with the chopped green onions.

SALMON BREAKFAST BOWL

For me, this Japanese-inspired breakfast is near-perfect eating. And by perfect, I mean pretty damn healthy and way delicious. You could eat it every single day.

2 teaspoons oil

¼ cup sliced yellow onion

1 large egg, beaten

1 cup leftover Perfectly Steamed Rice (page 218)

2 tablespoons finely diced green onion

2 tablespoons chopped fresh cilantro

2 tablespoons soy sauce

1 teaspoon sriracha

Juice of 1 lime wedge

3 ounces leftover Sesame Chili Salmon (page 156)

½ avocado, peeled, pitted, and diced

¼ cup toasted sliced almonds

Togarashi Japanese spice blend for garnish

1. Heat a medium nonstick skillet over medium-low heat and add the oil and onion. Cook until just softened, about 5 minutes.

2. Add the egg and cook over low heat until just set and not dry.

3. While it cooks, microwave the rice on HIGH in a microwave-safe bowl for about 30 seconds. Mix well with the green onion and cilantro and transfer to a soup-style bowl—unless you have a cool-looking Asian one like in the picture (I love this bowl, btw).

4. Combine the soy sauce, sriracha, and lime juice in a small bowl. Stir well, drizzle over the rice, and mix in.

5. Top with the salmon, avocado, egg, and almonds and sprinkle with togarashi.

FRIED RICE PANCAKES

MAKES ABOUT TEN 4-INCH PANCAKES

20 MINUTES

This is a sort of a mash-up between Chinese scallion pancakes and the popular Chinese street food *jianbing*. And although it ends up not really all that close to either one, these are still really good and rather addictive.

2 cups leftover Perfectly
   Steamed Rice (page 218)

1 cup prepared pancake mix
   (I use the "just add water" kind,
   but with 25% more water)

⅓ cup diced green onion,
   plus more for serving

⅓ cup finely shredded
   green cabbage

1 teaspoon sesame oil

Oil for pan

Hoisin sauce for serving

1. Heat a small nonstick pan over medium heat.

2. Combine the rice, prepared pancake batter, green onion, cabbage, and sesame oil in a large bowl and mix well.

3. Add the oil to the pan and, when hot, put in a ¼-cup scoop of the rice mixture and flatten with a spatula.

4. Cook for a couple of minutes, or until just set on the bottom, then flip and cook until done.

5. Brush with hoisin sauce and sprinkle with green onion before serving.

CHICKEN SOUP WITH RICE, LEMON & DILL

MAKES 4 TO 6 SERVINGS
20 MINUTES

My niece Lindsay will just not stop reminding me how good this is and how often she makes it. All right, already—it's in the book! Ya happy now?

2 tablespoons oil

2 celery stalks, sliced lengthwise down the middle, then crosswise into thin pieces

½ medium yellow onion, diced

8 cups chicken stock

2 cups leftover Perfectly Steamed Rice (page 218)

2 cups shredded leftover Perfect Roast Chicken (page 100)

1 cup packed fresh spinach leaves, roughly chopped

⅓ cup finely chopped fresh dill

1 teaspoon kosher salt

½ teaspoon freshly ground black pepper

Lemon wedges for serving

1. Heat the oil in a medium pot over medium heat, add the celery and onion, and cook until softened.

2. Add the stock (carefully cuz it'll steam) and bring to a simmer.

3. Then add the rice, chicken, spinach, and dill, stir, and let simmer until warmed, about 5 minutes.

4. Season with the salt and pepper.

5. Serve in bowls with a lemon wedge squeezed on top.

RICOTTA, BACON & ARUGULA PIZZA, AND THEN . . .

You can make something out of
leftover pizza besides leftover
pizza? Oh, you betcha.

Ricotta, Bacon & Arugula Pizza

Pizza Frittata

Pizza Eggs

Pizza Lasagna

Caesar

RICOTTA, BACON & ARUGULA PIZZA

MAKES ONE 12-INCH PIZZA
30 MINUTES

The point of this section, obviously, is to show how fricking diverse leftover pizza can be—any pizza. But I needed an example, and not only does this one make me very happy but it has all the right components for making the other things in this chapter.

5½ ounces bacon, thinly sliced crosswise

½ cup ricotta

1 tablespoon olive oil, plus more for arugula and pan

2 garlic cloves, minced

½ teaspoon red pepper flakes

1 to 2 cups packed baby arugula, or more depending on how arugula-y you like it

Kosher salt and freshly ground black pepper

1 ball pizza dough

½ cup shredded mozzarella

¼ cup grated Parmesan

1. Preheat the oven to 425°F. Lightly grease a baking sheet.

2. Cook the bacon until almost done but not quite yet crispy, then set aside.

3. Put the ricotta, oil, garlic, and red pepper flakes in a bowl and mix well until smooth, then set that aside, too.

4. Put the arugula in a large bowl, drizzle very lightly with oil, and season with a pinch of salt and black pepper to taste. Then, yep, set aside.

5. Stretch out the dough to 12 inches in diameter and put on the prepared baking sheet. Bake for 3 minutes.

6. Remove from the oven, spread with the ricotta mixture, top with the bacon, add the mozzarella and then the Parmesan.

7. Place back in the oven and bake for about 15 minutes more, or until starting to get brown, crispy, and bubbly.

8. Remove from the oven, top with the arugula and a few grinds of black pepper, and slice.

The Best Way to Perfectly Reheated Pizza

I don't like cold pizza. I also don't like shittily warmed pizza. And so, after extensive research, I believe I've perfected this reheating method. **MAKES AS MANY AS YOU WANT**

**Pizza slices, however much
  you need to reheat**

1. Heat a large nonstick skillet over medium-high heat.

2. Put the pizza slices on a microwave-safe plate—do not overcrowd.

3. Put the plate in a microwave on HIGH for . . . and this is the tricky part, because my microwave is a high-wattage one and cooks pretty quickly and yours might not be. (I'm not bragging, I'm just saying . . .) The goal is to nicely warm the toppings in the microwave, that's all . . . so maybe 30 seconds.

4. Remove carefully and immediately slide the slices (no more than three at a time) into the hot pan to crisp the bottom—crisping will take anywhere from 30 seconds to a minute.

5. Just remove, eat, and feel confident last night's pizza will be nearly as good today.

PIZZA FRITTATA

SERVES 6 TO 8
30 MINUTES

Okay, I like eggs . . . so sue me. Still, after a very late night with lots of "fun," if you know what I mean, you wake up the next morning and suddenly realize that:

- *the place looks like shit*
- *somebody's parents are coming for brunch*
- *there are three or four slices of a giant pepperoni/ mushroom/artichoke pizza sitting on the coffee table that no one can remember ordering*

What do you do? You take a breath, you put someone on mixing Caesars (Canadian Bloody Marys; page 239), you get someone making a big-ass salad, you set the oven to 300°F, and you make this easy frittata that'll be delicious and, more important, impress the hell outta the parents.

2 tablespoons oil

½ cup diced onion (any onion will work—green, red, yellow . . .)

1 big ol' garlic clove, minced

2 cups roughly chopped leftover pizza

2 big handfuls baby spinach or arugula

10 large eggs, beaten

½ cup shredded Monterey Jack

Kosher salt and freshly ground black pepper

1. Preheat the oven to 300°F.

2. Put a large, ovenproof skillet over medium heat and add the oil and the onion. Cook about 3 minutes and then add the garlic and chopped pizza.

3. Cook for about 3 minutes, stirring often, and put in the spinach.

4. Stirring constantly, cook until wilted, about 2 minutes, then add the eggs, cheese, and salt and pepper to taste.

5. When the bottom starts to set, transfer the pan to the oven and let firm up—this might take 15 to 20 minutes.

PIZZA EGGS

Fine, I'll admit it. This was probably created somewhere around 4:20 one morning. That being said, it's damn fricking good anytime. And depending on your slice, it could already have cheese, veggies, meat, etc.—it's a no-brainer.

1 decent slice pizza—and by "decent," I don't mean a giant slice, nor do I mean a tiny little piece like out of a Lunchables box

1 tablespoon butter

2 large eggs, beaten

Kosher salt and freshly ground black pepper

1. Rough chop the pizza slice into about 1-inch pieces.

2. Heat the butter in a small nonstick skillet over medium heat and add the pizza pieces.

3. Stir until heated through, then add the eggs and season with salt and pepper.

4. Now just cook like basic scrambled eggs until done—or pushed over to one side with over easy eggs.

5. Eat and smile.

PIZZA LASAGNA

What I like about this is that people will assume it's lasagna with pizzalike ingredients and flavors. And when you tell them it's actually lasagna made out of pizza slices, they're stumped . . . and you're a genius.

10 ounces ricotta

2 tablespoons olive oil

1 large garlic clove, minced

The equivalent of about a 12-inch leftover pizza

1⅓ cups leftover Roasted Red Pepper Sauce (page 180)

1 cup shredded mozzarella

⅓ cup shredded Parmesan

1. Preheat the oven to 350°F.

2. Combine the ricotta with the oil and garlic in a medium bowl and mix well.

3. Cut the pizza into thin strips—any length is fine.

4. Spread about 1/3 cup of the red pepper sauce on the bottom of an 8-inch square baking dish, then scatter with one-third of the pizza strips, then one-third of the ricotta mixture and one-third of the mozzarella. Repeat twice.

5. Add the last of the red pepper sauce and top with the Parmesan.

6. Cover with foil, bake for 30 minutes, remove the foil, and bake for 10 minutes more, or until heated through and bubbly.

7. Remove from the oven and let sit for 10 minutes before cutting into it.

CAESAR

I realize this isn't leftover from anything really, but this Canadian Bloody Mary is so good, it would have been mean of me not to include it—especially in a chapter with two egg-based recipes.

1½ tablespoons celery salt

1 tablespoon freshly ground black pepper

1 lime

4 ounces tomato-clam juice, such as Clamato (you'll find it in the store with the tomato juice—and before you get all squirrely thinking it'll just taste like a bucket of clams, it doesn't)

4 ounces vodka

1 teaspoon Worcestershire sauce

2 teaspoons prepared horseradish

4 good dashes of hot sauce; I like Cholula

1. Put 1 tablespoon of the celery salt and the pepper on a small plate and mix together.

2. Slice a wedge of lime and rub around the rim of two glasses. Slice off two more wedges for garnish.

3. Rim the glasses with the salt mixture.

4. Fill a shaker one-quarter full with ice and add the tomato-clam juice, vodka, Worcestershire, horseradish, hot sauce, remaining 1½ teaspoons of celery salt, and a squeeze of juice from the rest of the lime.

5. Shake well and pour over fresh ice into glasses, being careful not to disturb the rimmed edge.

6. Drop in a lime wedge, sit back, and enjoy.

7. Oh, and an urge to quietly hum "O Canada" is quite normal.

5-MINUTE BEER BREAD, AND THEN . . .

Okay, so although it takes only
about 5 minutes to make, it takes
an hour to cook. That being said,
you get the all-important smell
of baking bread that makes it
almost worth it just for that.
But once it's made . . .

5-Minute Beer Bread
Panzanella Eggs
Whiskey Bread Pudding
French Toast Mountain
Garlic Croutons
Compound Butters

5-MINUTE BEER BREAD

MAKES 1 LOAF

ABOUT 75 MINUTES

I'm not a baker and likely never will be. But someone showed me this dog-simple recipe years ago, and while I'm still not a baker, I now can make a simple, great loaf of bread . . . and so can you.

4 tablespoons (½ stick) butter, melted

3 cups self-rising flour

3 tablespoons sugar

One 12-ounce bottle beer, preferably something with a little flavor, at room temperature

½ cup diced green chiles (optional)

1 cup diced cooked bacon (optional)

1. Preheat the oven to 350°F.

2. Butter a 9-by-5-inch loaf pan well with half of the butter.

3. Put the flour and sugar in a large bowl and mix well. Slowly pour in the beer.

4. Stir everything together (this is the time to add either or both of the optional ingredients), and mix until well combined. Pour into the prepared loaf pan.

5. Melt the remaining butter and pour over the top.

6. Bake in the center of the oven for about 50 minutes, or until a skewer comes out clean when poked into the center of the loaf and pulled out.

7. Remove from the oven and, using oven mitts, carefully invert the pan to release loaf onto a wire rack. Allow to cool for 10 minutes before eating—if you can wait.

PANZANELLA EGGS

SERVES 1
10 MINUTES

A panzanella salad is an Italian-style salad with dressing, soaked day-old bread, tomatoes, and onions. This is not that. This is its much more fun egg cousin that you'll love so much you'll want to marry it. Which is illegal, I believe, except for maybe in Utah.

1 tablespoon oil

1 tablespoon butter

⅓ cup torn or cubed leftover 5-Minute Beer Bread (page 242)

2 tablespoons diced onion (red, yellow, green, or white—they're all good)

2 large eggs

Kosher salt and freshly ground pepper

2 tablespoons shredded Monterey Jack

1. Heat a small nonstick skillet over medium heat and add the oil and butter.

2. When they've melted, put in the bread and onion and stir to coat.

3. When the onion softens and the bread starts to get crispy on the edges, lower the heat a little and add the eggs, salt, and pepper.

4. Stirring slowly, cook the eggs and, when they're about half set, add the cheese.

5. Continue to cook, stirring, until done. Plate and, well, you know what to do next.

WHISKEY BREAD PUDDING

SERVES 8
1 HOUR

Cuz why not? Btw, it's not really bread and it's not really pudding.

2 tablespoons butter
   for casserole dish
1 loaf leftover 5-Minute Beer
   Bread (page 242), ends
   sliced off and discarded,
   cut into 1-inch cubes
¾ cup pecan pieces
½ cup chocolate chips
3 large eggs
2 cups half-and-half
1¾ cups milk
¾ cup sugar
¼ cup whiskey—this is not the
   place for 18-year-old Jameson;
   an inexpensive one will be fine
Whipped cream for serving

1. Preheat the oven to 350°F.

2. Lightly butter a 9-inch square casserole dish.

3. Put the bread cubes on the bottom of the prepared casserole dish.

4. Scatter ½ cup of the pecans and all of the chocolate chips over the bread.

5. Mix together the eggs, half-and-half, milk, sugar, and whiskey in a medium bowl and pour over the bread.

6. Lightly push down with a fork until the bread is covered and soaking up the egg mixture.

7. Bake for 30 to 45 minutes, until the top springs back when lightly tapped.

8. Remove from the oven, let cool slightly, and serve in bowls with whipped cream topped with the remaining pecans.

FRENCH TOAST MOUNTAIN

SERVES 2 OR 3

15 MINUTES

I've been making this forever. Originally for my kids, and later on for anyone, just because it's fun.

3 large eggs

3 tablespoons milk

1 tablespoon sugar

1 tablespoon ground cinnamon

About 2 tablespoons butter for every couple pieces of bread

6 slices leftover 5-Minute Beer Bread (page 242)

6 slices bacon, cooked until crispy and chopped into small pieces

Pure maple or pancake syrup

Powdered sugar

1. Beat the eggs in a wide bowl, add the milk, sugar, and cinnamon, and mix well.

2. Heat a large nonstick skillet or flat griddle over medium heat and add the butter.

3. When the butter has melted, dip the bread into the egg mixture and place in the pan—so far, just like regular French toast.

4. Cook until goldeny-brown or beginning to get slightly crispy—still like French toast.

5. Remove from the heat, cut into 1-inch squares, and divide between two plates, forming a tall, mountainlike pile on each plate. Top each with some bacon.

6. Drizzle with syrup and dust with powdered sugar—this is the cascading waterfall and snowy peaks part.

GARLIC CROUTONS

MAKES 2 CUPS CROUTONS

10 MINUTES

Croutons are often dried out—but not these. These croutons are rich, buttery, crispy, and delicious.

2 tablespoons olive oil

2 tablespoons butter

2 cups leftover 5-Minute Beer Bread (page 242), torn or chopped into bite-size pieces

Kosher salt and freshly ground black pepper

½ teaspoon garlic powder

A sprinkle of fresh parsley or cilantro (optional)

1. Heat a large skillet over medium-low heat and add the oil and butter.

2. When they've melted, put in the bread and stir to coat. Then add a good pinch of salt, pepper to taste, the garlic powder, and the parsley or cilantro (if using) and stir again.

3. Keeping the croutons moving in the pan, cook for 5 to 6 minutes, until crispy and golden.

COMPOUND BUTTERS

While more "newover" than "leftover," this is one of the greatest things you can keep in your fridge. Oh, and only the ingredients change; the directions are the same for all three of them. Turn the page to see how tasty they look.

JALAPEÑO CILANTRO:

8 tablespoons (1 stick) butter,
   at room temperature

1 teaspoon minced
   jalapeño pepper

2 teaspoons chopped
   fresh cilantro

1 garlic clove, minced

CHIPOTLE:

8 tablespoons (1 stick) butter,
   at room temperature

1 garlic clove, minced

2 chipotle chiles, finely minced

2 tablespoons minced
   fresh cilantro

Juice of ½ lime

Kosher salt and freshly
   ground black pepper

GARLIC LEMON HERB:

8 tablespoons (1 stick) butter,
   at room temperature

3 tablespoons finely chopped
   mixed fresh herbs—parsley,
   cilantro, thyme, rosemary, etc.

Zest of ½ lemon

1 large garlic clove, finely minced

Pinch of kosher salt

1. Put all the ingredients for your compound of choice in a bowl and mix well to combine.

2. Place on plastic wrap and roll into a log, twisting the ends to seal it well.

3. Refrigerate for at least an hour, then use. Compound butter can keep refrigerated for up to a month, or in the freezer for about 3 months.

Jalapeño Butter

Cilantro Butter

Garlic Lemon Herb
Butter

INDEX